"The Lord has called the whole family of God to come and sing together to him. This book will help tune our hearts to do that!"

Keith and Kristyn Getty, hymn writers, "In Christ Alone"

"*Sunday Matters* is a book that matters. In this brilliant new devotional, Paul Tripp encourages us not to give up the habit of meeting together—reminding us just how profound a gift our corporate worship can be. In recent times many around the world had the blessing of the gathered church temporarily taken away. As we bounced back, we remembered once again that we are better together, and we treasured the unparalleled dynamic of the living God dwelling among his people. We were never made to go 'lone ranger'—that's not how the kingdom of God works—and this book is a beautiful and timely reminder of that. Tripp is an inspiring writer, and each of these fifty-two chapters will lead you deeper into the glory of the gathered church."

Matt Redman, worship leader; songwriter, "10,000 Reasons (Bless the Lord)"

"Each act of corporate worship serves to help God's people rehearse and remember the goodness of the gospel. From the call to worship to the benediction, we need a greater understanding of what we are doing when we gather and why we do it. *Sunday Matters* has helped me see with fresh eyes the beauty and wonder of corporate worship, and I pray it does the same for you."

Matt Boswell, hymn writer; Pastor, The Trails Church, Celina, Texas; Assistant Professor of Church Music and Worship, The Southern Baptist Theological Seminary

"Getting myself and our three young sons out the door to church was pure chaos at times. Tears and yelling were often involved, from me more than them. Paul David Tripp helps every single one of us remember why going to church matters and how to prepare our hearts to worship and encounter Jesus there each week. I wish I had this book years ago! This is a gift for you and your whole family."

Ann Wilson, Cohost, *FamilyLife Today*; author, *Vertical Marriage* and *No Perfect Parents*

Sunday Matters

Books by Paul David Tripp

40 Days of Faith
40 Days of Grace
40 Days of Hope
40 Days of Love
A Quest for More: Living for Something Bigger Than You
A Shelter in the Time of Storm: Meditations on God and Trouble
Age of Opportunity: A Biblical Guide for Parenting Teens
Awe: Why It Matters for Everything We Think, Say, and Do
Broken-Down House: Living Productively in a World Gone Bad
Come, Let Us Adore Him: A Daily Advent Devotional
Dangerous Calling: Confronting the Unique Challenges of Pastoral Ministry
Do You Believe: 12 Historic Doctrines to Change Your Everyday Life
Forever: Why You Can't Live without It
How People Change (with Timothy S. Lane)
*Instruments in the Redeemer's Hands: People in Need of Change Helping
   People in Need of Change*
Journey to the Cross: A 40-Day Lenten Devotional
Lead: 12 Gospel Principles for Leadership in the Church
Lost in the Middle: Midlife and the Grace of God
Marriage: 6 Gospel Commitments Every Couple Needs to Make
My Heart Cries Out: Gospel Meditations for Everyday Life
New Morning Mercies: A Daily Gospel Devotional
Parenting: 14 Gospel Principles That Can Radically Change Your Family
Reactivity: How the Gospel Transforms Our Actions and Reactions
Redeeming Money: How God Reveals and Reorients Our Hearts
Relationships: A Mess Worth Making (with Timothy S. Lane)
Sex in a Broken World: How Christ Redeems What Sin Distorts
Suffering: Gospel Hope When Life Doesn't Make Sense
Sunday Matters: 52 Devotionals to Prepare Your Heart for Church
War of Words: Getting to the Heart of Your Communication Struggles
Whiter Than Snow: Meditations on Sin and Mercy

Sunday Matters

52 Devotionals to Prepare Your Heart for Church

Paul David Tripp

WHEATON, ILLINOIS

Library of Congress Cataloging-in-Publication Data
Names: Tripp, Paul David, 1950– author.
Title: Sunday matters : 52 devotionals to prepare your heart for church / Paul David Tripp.
Description: Wheaton, Illinois : Crossway, 2023. | Includes bibliographical references and index.
Identifiers: LCCN 2023000660 (print) | LCCN 2023000661 (ebook) | ISBN 9781433582820 (hardcover) | ISBN 9781433582837 (pdf) | ISBN 9781433582851 (epub)
Subjects: LCSH: Public worship—Prayers and devotions.
Classification: LCC BV15 .T75 2023 (print) | LCC BV15 (ebook) | DDC 264—dc23/eng/20230420
LC record available at https://lccn.loc.gov/2023000660
LC ebook record available at https://lccn.loc.gov/2023000661

Crossway is a publishing ministry of Good News Publishers.

LSC		32	31	30	29	28	27	26	25	24	23
15	14	13	12	11	10	9	8	7	6	5	4	3	2	1

To all the pastors whose words Sunday after Sunday have caused me to fall in love with the gospel and the Savior, who is the hero of its hope.

Introduction

LIKE EVERY HUMAN BEING, I grew up in a less-than-perfect family. But one positive thing my family did marked me forever. Every Saturday night my siblings and I, one after the other, would take a bath and then deliver our shoes to my dad to be polished, all in preparation for the Sunday morning worship service at the Toledo Gospel Tabernacle. There was never a debate about whether we would be going. There was no need to fit church into the family schedule. The weekend schedule of the Tripp family was planned around the one thing that we would never think of missing: Sunday worship.

For that, I will be forever grateful.

It seemed like we were always the first family to arrive. My dad hated being late for church. And because he had lost much of his hearing in World War II, we always sat right up front so he could hear. I heard well over a thousand sermons, preached from all over God's word. I learned all of the great hymns of the faith, many of which I can still sing by memory. I learned the core doctrines of the faith as I sat there with Mom and Dad. I grew up thinking that "going to church" was a normal part of life. It didn't seem religious to me or superspiritual or some kind of unique commitment. From my youngest days, it seemed to me to be a thing that all Christian families did. For my family there was no exception to this Sunday rule. Even when we were on vacation, my mom and dad would locate a church for us to attend. I am so thankful for the way this important spiritual habit was nailed into my understanding of life.

But as I look back, I don't think my mom and dad ever talked about preparing our hearts for worship. The conscious and intentional worship of God is the highest calling and most wonderful thing a human being could ever do and, because it is, it is a location for spiritual war. That war is fought on the ground of our hearts. The enemy of our souls will do anything he can to keep us from participating fully, from hearing clearly, and from committing to God more intentionally through gathered worship. It is easy to enter worship unready. I remember my mom and dad arguing on the way to church, which resulted in all of us walking into that big building riled up inside. I remember crying in the car because I thought my worn-out shoes looked silly, and then thinking about it throughout the whole service. I remember as a teenager being more excited about meeting a girl at church than I was about meeting with my Lord.

Maybe you're distracted by unpaid bills, with no plan to be able to pay them. Maybe you hit Sunday morning with a struggle to trust God because he doesn't seem near or caring. Maybe marriage coldness and conflict make it hard for you to go to worship without being distracted by all those happy couples around you. Perhaps you come with a struggle with the leadership or direction of your church. Maybe you're going through a period of coldness of heart. It could be that success and power have become more attractive to you than a life that pleases God. Maybe physical weakness makes the whole experience unpleasant and uncomfortable. Perhaps you're brokenhearted at the spiritual state of your children, so much so that it's hard to think about anything else. It could be that your job has gotten you down and has become a huge thought burden to you. Maybe you're grieving a miscarriage, the loss of a loved one, the demise of a lifelong dream, the betrayal of a friend, disappointment with God, or a significant family trauma. Maybe self-righteousness and self-sufficiency have diminished your hunger for what gathered worship has to offer. Or perhaps the gospel doesn't captivate and excite you as it once did.

The fact that we are God's children doesn't give us a ticket out of the harsh realities of life in this sin-broken world. Somehow, someway that brokenness will enter each of our doors. The Bible tells us that between the "already" of our conversion and the "not yet" of our homegoing, we will all face temptation and we will all groan. Life right here, right now is often burdensome and hard. So we tend to carry our burdens with us, like the heavy backpack of a young school student, and these burdens often distract us from the richness of corporate worship.

All of this means that often on Sunday morning we're not spiritually ready for the profoundly important thing we're about to do: offer to our Lord the worship that he deserves and open our hearts to instruction from his word. We often don't approach gathered worship with joyful, grateful, and expectant hearts. So I offer this to you. Here are fifty-two brief devotionals to help prepare your heart for the beauty of what Sunday worship has to offer you. My prayer is not just that this preparation will help you to be able to more fully participate in God's wonderful gift of corporate worship, but more importantly that your continual participation will transform your relationship with your Lord and the way you live your life. May this devotional cause that weekly formal corporate worship to spill over into your daily life, so that your life becomes a hymn of worship to the Savior who rescued you, adopted you, and daily works to draw you near.

Sunday 1

*Corporate worship is designed to remind you
again and again that the most valuable thing
in your life you could have never earned or
deserved; it was and is a gift of divine grace.*

I DON'T KNOW ABOUT YOU, but in the rush and press of life
I can lose my mind. No, I'm not talking about going insane and
needing to be institutionalized. I'm talking about a much more
subtle form of insanity that often inflicts me and a vast number
of my Christian brothers and sisters. There are moments in my
life when I lose my gospel mind. There are moments when I live
as if God does not exist, the Bible had never been written, and
Jesus had never lived, died, and rose again. I'm not referencing
an intentional walking away from the faith but rather a deformative gospel forgetfulness. Why do I call it *deformative*? Because in
these moments my life is no longer formed by a vibrant rest in a
surrender to my Lord but rather it is deformed by other things
in and around me. There are times when I lose sight of what is
truly important and valuable in life and, when I do, it alters what

I desire, how I think, what I say, and the things I do. I am sure I am not alone.

Perhaps during an argument with your husband, wife, or friend, securing affirmation as being right (for once) becomes the most important thing to you. You have lost your gospel mind. Maybe you find yourself doing whatever is necessary to get that job promotion. You have lost your gospel mind. Maybe you're willing to destroy your relationship with your neighbor over a boundary dispute. You have lost your gospel mind. Maybe you rip vengefully into your teenager because you're tired of being disrespected. You have lost your gospel mind. Maybe you cling to an unending obsession with your weight and appearance. You have lost your gospel mind. Perhaps a lifestyle dream is leading you into crushing debt. You have lost your gospel mind. Maybe you harbor a pattern of internet sexual sin. You have lost your gospel mind. Maybe you feel an overwhelming anxiety about what people think about you and how they respond to you. You have lost your gospel mind. Or you might demand to be in charge and in control of your relationships. You have lost your gospel mind. Maybe you are passive and complacent when it comes to your faith. You have lost your gospel mind. Maybe patterns of envy and bitterness have robbed you of your joy. You have lost your gospel mind.

Because the radical, life-shaping, and hope-giving values of the gospel are nowhere reinforced in the surrounding culture, we all live in constant need of fundamental gospel-values clarification. We all need to be reminded again and again of what is truly valuable and, therefore, what should be truly formative in life. I'm sure you are aware that it has never been more difficult to keep the worldly, materialistic, and degospelized values of the culture around us at bay. It is harder than ever to quiet the cacophony of voices and think with gospel clarity about what is truly important. It's hard because we now carry in our pockets or purses all of those voices in a single piece of powerful technology. It is nearly impossible to overstate the influence of Twitter, TikTok, Instagram, Facebook, and other social media on how we think about ourselves and life itself. In those moments when you're not actively doing something, it's hard not to reach down, pull out the device, and surf once again. It's hard not to feel the need to post your life, and then compare your life to others who are posting their lives. Meanwhile, it's hard to see the ways in which these powerful habits of influence have caused you to forget what is truly valuable in life.

But as is true with every other spiritual danger in our lives, God, in grace, meets us at our point of need with just what we need. What is one of the primary ways our loving Savior meets us as we struggle not to lose our gospel minds? He meets us with the gift of his church. He knows that we need help. He knows we are not spiritually hardwired to make it on our own. So he has ordained his church to regularly gather, that we would remember once again, grieve once again, celebrate once again, and go out and live in light of the beautiful values of the gospel of Jesus Christ. These regular gatherings of God's people are not first an obligation; they are a gift. They are not first a duty; they are a welcome. They are the Father pulling you up on his lap, whispering in your ear that he loves you, reminding you of who you are and of the surpassing value of being in his family, and then putting you down and sending you on your way.

The regular gathering of the church is designed to lovingly confront us with the fact that the most valuable thing in life can't be earned. The most valuable thing in life cannot be humanly achieved. The most valuable thing is life can't be purchased or owned. The most valuable thing in life is not an experience you will have. The most valuable thing in life is not something you will get from people in your life. The most valuable thing in life is an eternal gift of divine grace. It is my eternal forgiveness, my eternal acceptance into the family of God, and the guaranteed destiny that is mine as a child of God, all secured for me by the righteous life, substitutionary death, and life-giving resurrection of Jesus. The most valuable thing in all of life is my union with Christ. By grace, he is in me and I am in him. This union means I don't have to be spiritually and emotionally imprisoned by past regrets, I don't have to live fearfully and powerlessly in the present, and I don't have to be crippled by anxiety in the future. Gospel values allow me to live at the intersection of humility and hope. They allow me to live with a radical honesty about my own weaknesses while living with courage as well. They lead me to live for a glory greater than my own, to be generous as God has been generous to me, to forgive as I have been forgiven, and to pursue growth in spiritual maturity more than I pursue any other kind of success in my life. No, I don't mean that I quit doing all the things that every other human being must do (job, relationships, finances, physical health, entertainment and leisure). Rather, these domains of my life take on new meaning and purpose because they are no longer the places where I look for life, but are now the places where I joyfully live out the life that I have been given by redeeming grace alone.

May we look with anticipation to the weekly gathering as a gift, just as we would look with anticipation at opening a gift handed to us by a loved one. Corporate worship is God's weekly gift to us, wrapped in the grace of Jesus and given by the one who created us, knows us, understands the temptations that greet us in the broken world we live in, and offers us the help we need. This gathering reminds us that God will never grow tired of us, never regret that we are in his family, and never walk away in disgust. No, he welcomes us to gather once again, and in gathering to remember, and in remembering to have our values clarified, and in having our values clarified to have the worship of our hearts reclaimed and our living reordered. May we receive his gift of the gathering of his church with joy, "not neglecting to meet together, as is the habit of some, but encouraging one another, and all the more as you see the Day drawing near" (Heb. 10:25).

Scripture: Matthew 6:19–21 and 13:44–46

Reflections: What habit are you tempted to lose your *gospel mind* to, and how can regularly gathering with God's people remedy that? To whom or what do you tend to look for *life*?

Family Discussion: Read the above Scripture passages and ask family members to name something that worshiping should remind us of (e.g., the extraordinary value of the gospel). Ask children to name some gifts they have received this year. Discuss how corporate worship is God's weekly gift to us, and how it is so much more valuable than other gifts.

Sunday 2

Corporate worship is designed to encourage you to cry for help to the one who always knows exactly what you need and who will meet you with boundless love, infinite wisdom, incalculable power, and inexhaustible grace.

ALL TOO OFTEN we find it hard to reach out for help. Yes, we know we weren't designed to go it alone and we know we are less than perfect, but we still hesitate to say, "I'm not doing well, and I need help." Often pride props up an external veneer that keeps those around us thinking we're doing just fine, when we are not fine. Pride makes us want to project that we are mature, wise, and capable. So when asked how we're doing, we'll give platitudinous non-answers like "Things have been tough, but the Lord is good." Or we'll give situational answers to personal questions. Someone asks us how we are, and we say, "It's been a rough week." Notice that there is no personal information there. You have talked about the situation, but not about how you are doing in dealing with it. All this keeps us from getting the help that we all need.

The reality is that each one of us is unfinished, still in the middle of God's lifelong work of maturing and transforming grace. We all live in a broken world that is groaning, waiting for redemption (Rom. 8:22–23). We all face things that God has brought into our lives that we would have never chosen or planned for ourselves. So we all face moments when we feel unprepared, confused, inadequate, disappointed, grieved, or fearful, and we're not sure how to think about or respond to what is now on our plate. We all know that we fall short of God's holy standard. We all know that there is more for us to learn and understand about God's will and plan for us. We all know that we still need to do a better job of living in light of what we say we believe. Perhaps your marriage is more of a struggle that you thought it would ever be. Maybe you're overwhelmed at the task of making sure your disabled child has every resource he needs. Or maybe there's a heartbreaking conflict in your extended family. Perhaps things in your life have caused you to silently doubt the goodness of God. Maybe as a Christian in a secular university you are tired of being misjudged, misunderstood, and mocked for your faith. Maybe you've been hurt by your church, and you don't know what to do next. Or you may be living with the sting of the disloyalty of someone you thought was your best friend. Maybe you're confronting the physical and relational trials of old age. The reality is that all of us need help all of the time.

To be human is to need help. Think of Adam and Eve. God created them with no physical or spiritual flaws; they were perfect. Not only that, but they lived in a completely perfect world where everything was in its right place, doing what God created it to do. And to top it all off, they were living in a perfect relationship with God. You would think they couldn't possibly be needy, but they were, because God did not design them to live independently of him or of one another. Healthy independent living is a delusion. So, immediately upon creating Adam and Eve, God talked to them because they did not understand who they were and how they were designed to live. Only in a life of submission to, fellowship with, and dependence upon their Creator would Adam and Eve be what they were supposed to be and do what they were designed to do. They were perfect people in a perfect world and in perfect relationship with God, but they still needed help. We need help not just because we are sinners or failures in some way, but because we are beings designed by a wise, loving, and good God for dependent living. You don't have to regret your need for help. It should not make you feel guilty. You shouldn't let shame keep you from seeking the help you need. You shouldn't let pride, the fear of what people will think, or how others will respond keep you from seeking the help that not only *you* need, but that everyone around you needs as well.

Here's the good news. The best help ever is available to you as a child of God. It's not a help that comes from your spouse, neighbor, friend, pastor, coworker, parent, or counselor. No, there is someone who always knows exactly what you need, when you need it, and how it is best delivered. This means that you are never caught in a situation where you are completely without help. One of the purposes of the weekly gatherings of the community of faith is to encourage us to confront our fear and pride and to comfort us with the fact that we have a Father who knows just what we need and who has lovingly committed himself to meet those needs. The gathering of the church is not an assembly of religiously independent people celebrating our successes, all dressed up parading ourselves before one another and before God. No, the church is the gathering of the needy, the weak, the broken, and the confused. But we are eternally loved and accepted by the one we worship and entrust ourselves to. We gather because we are not okay and we need to remember that God is for us, in us, and with us and, because he is, we have glorious hope and help in our time of need.

The words of Philippians 4:19 get me up in the morning: "And my God will supply every need of yours according to his riches in glory in Christ Jesus." Consider, too, what Peter says as he writes to suffering people: "His divine power has granted to us all things that pertain to life and godliness" (2 Pet. 1:3). God promised to supply everything we need not only for eternal life but for godliness. What is godliness? It is a God-honoring life between the "already" of our conversion and the "not yet" of our homegoing. Peter is talking about God's ready supply of divine resources to meet our need for help right here, right now in the place where we are living and with regard to the challenges we are facing. Reflect also on what Paul writes near the end of his treatise on suffering in Romans 8: "What then shall we say to these things? If God is for us, who can be against us? He who did not spare his own Son but gave him up for us all, how will he not also with him graciously give us all things?" (8:31–32). The cross of Jesus Christ is our guarantee that the one who met us at our greatest point of need (our sin) will continue to supply what we need. If he went to this extent to meet the need of needs, would it make any sense for him to abandon us now?

The regular gathering of the church is the assembly of God's needy children. This gathering is a welcome to lay down our pride, our self-sufficiency, our delusions of independent strength, our fear of what others will think, and our self-righteousness, and to humbly open our hearts, confessing our need once again to the one who has the power and willingness to help. We gather once again to be reminded of how this willing God meets us.

God meets us with mercies that are always new.

God meets us with boundless love.

God meets us with infinite wisdom.

God meets us with incalculable power.

God meets us with inexhaustible grace.

And because he does, we do not need to let fear, guilt, or shame paralyze us. I know that I need that reminder again and again. So, this Sunday gather with your needy brothers and sisters. Lift up your hands in faith and reach out for your Father's help and drink in all the reminders in song and word that he is good, kind, loving, and faithful. And with a joyful heart remember once more that he cares about his children and will never turn his back on their needs.

———

Scripture: Psalm 54:4 and Hebrews 4:16

Reflections: In a culture that encourages independence and even isolation, how can we begin to practice humble dependence upon God?

Family Discussion: Read aloud Hebrews 4:16 and discuss who we can turn to when we need help. What is the *throne of grace* and who is seated on it? Talk about any barriers in life that might deter you from asking for help.

Sunday 3

Corporate worship is designed by God to give you eyes to see, a mind to understand, and an open heart to receive the bad news of the gospel (sin) and the good news of the gospel (grace) in ways that transform your heart.

ONE OF THE PROBLEMS with the internet and the intrusive power of social media is the constant onslaught of bad news. We no longer carry the hardships of just our personal life, but we are daily greeted by every bad thing that happens around the world. Wars are fought before us in real time; battle scenes, with their destruction and gore, instantly become videos on our Twitter feeds. It's hard to avoid the darkness of the culture around us, the anger of people, and the constant telling and retelling of hard things that are out of our control. I think we carry a burden of fear and dread unlike what has ever been carried before, because we are exposed to more sad things than people have ever been before. It wears on us. It is exhausting and disheartening. It makes us feel small, the victims of things we now carry but have no ability to change. In fact, I recently told my wife, Luella, that I was tired of all the bad news and I wanted to watch something mindless that would give my weary brain a break.

However, there is one kind of bad news that you and I often work to deny but that we desperately need to face. Facing this news is a matter of life and death, even though it is the worst news ever. Willingness to open your heart to this deeply bad news will set your life on a gloriously new trajectory that literally has no end. This is bad news that you and I need to hear. Without this news we will fail to understand ourselves, our relationships, and the world we live in. Most importantly we will fail to understand the deep need we have for what the person and work of Jesus can offer us.

We need to hear, understand, and accept the bad news of our sin. I find David's description of sin, in his heartfelt confession in Psalm 51, to be very helpful. Here he describes sin with three words: *transgression*, *iniquity*, and *sin*. *Transgression* is a willing stepping over of God's boundaries. It is like parking in the no-parking zone even though I've seen the sign. It is a pattern of choosing what you want to do even though it violates what God has commanded you to do. Sadly, apart from divine rescue, this spirit of rebellion lurks in all of our hearts. The word *iniquity* pictures moral uncleanness. Think of water that has alien chemicals in it that will hurt you if not purified. *Iniquity* tells me that sin is not just a behavioral problem, something that I do, but more foundationally it is a heart problem; it is something that I am. My deepest problem, apart from God's grace, is not just that I do sinful things but that I am a sinner. Because sin is part of my nature, I cannot escape it on my own. I can run from situations and people, but I cannot run from myself. The rhetorical question of Jeremiah is helpful here:

Can the Ethiopian change his skin
    or the leopard his spots?
Then also you can do good
    who are accustomed to evil. (Jer. 13:23)

The Ethiopian is dark-skinned by nature, and like any human being, he has no ability to change his skin color. If he dyed his skin, a new layer of skin would grow in his natural color. The leopard is spotted, and even if you shaved that leopard clean, its spots would grow back. So it is with sin. Since it is a matter of our nature, we have no ability to escape it and, therefore, no ability on our own to live a consistently good life in the eyes of God.

The word *sin* is meant to picture our inability. Sin renders us lame and weak, constantly falling below God's holy, wise, and loving standard. Imagine spending a hundred years with a bow in your hand, trying to hit a target, and every time you launch an arrow, it falls short. Despite your best intentions and efforts, nothing changes; your arrows always fall short. So it is with sin. Sin makes it impossible for us to live up to the standard of who the Creator designed us to be and what he designed us to do. These three words—*transgression*, *iniquity*, and *sin*—powerfully depict our need for the rescuing, forgiving, accepting, transforming, empowering, and delivering grace of the Lord Jesus Christ. They should cause us to give up on our own righteousness, to let go of our dreams of self-reformation, and to cry out for help. These words should drive us to a state of spiritual hopelessness that causes us to abandon hope in our efforts and throw ourselves in hope on the Savior.

But we have a problem. One of the most serious aspects of sin is that it is deceitful. Sin blinds. I have no problem seeing and being concerned about the sin of others, but I can be blind to my own sin and a bit offended when someone calls me out. It is vital to admit that because sin still lives inside of us, none of us have a completely accurate view of ourselves. We like to think that no one knows us better than we know ourselves, but the blinding power of sin means that simply is not true. But it's also vital to understand that sin carries with it a double blindness; not only am I often blind to my sin, but I am often blind to my blindness. I look at myself like I'm looking in carnival mirrors, where I see myself but with significant distortions. I need help to see myself accurately, to grieve, and to seek and celebrate God's redeeming grace.

Corporate worship, the regular gathering of God's people, holds up a huge mirror week after week. It is the world's most accurate mirror, one that doesn't simply give us an accurate view of our physical appearance but that has the power to reveal and expose the true thoughts, desires, and condition of our hearts. What is this mirror? It is the word of God. The Scripture read, sung, and expounded functions, in the hands of the Holy Spirit, as a mirror, enabling us to see ourselves as we really are, so that we will seek the grace that we deeply need. Because of remaining sin, we need this heart-exposing ministry again and again. I am thankful that week after week, God has used the corporate gathering for worship as an instrument of accurate spiritual sightedness in my life.

Why do I need this regular flow of bad news? Because without it, the good news of the righteous life, substitutionary death, and victorious resurrection of Jesus would neither interest me nor seem important to me. It is the crushing bad news of sin that causes me to long for the gloriously good news of all that Jesus has done, is doing, and will do for me. It makes me cling to his grace because I know I have no other hope in this life and in the one to come.

And it makes me want to extend that same grace to those around me who likewise have no hope without it.

This Sunday once again stand before God's mirror. Let it break through your blindness, let it expose your need, and let it cause you to throw yourself once again into the healing, forgiving, and restoring arms of your Savior.

———

Scripture: Jeremiah 17:9–10

Reflections: Why is it so difficult to recognize our own sin? How can we see ourselves as we really are, and why is it important to do so?

Family Discussion: Read aloud Jeremiah 17:9–10. Ask what this verse means when it says that the heart is *deceitful*. Discuss whether or not a mirror is useful if it doesn't show what we really look like. Discuss whether it is enough to look in a mirror just once in our lives. Why not? Compare this to weekly worship which, through the word of God, shows us our sin and extends grace to us.

Sunday 4

Corporate worship is designed to turn your fear into trust, your complaints into praise, and your independence into willing submission.

I WISH I COULD SAY that I always perfectly trust and rest in the Lord. I wish I could say that everything I do is rooted in faith and not in fear. I wish I could say that everything I do and say is shaped by a willing submission to God's will. I wish I could say all of these things, but I can't. In my sane moments I am able to see that there is still spiritual struggle within me, that the desire for my own way collides with my commitment to live God's way. Sometimes I am confused about what God is doing, when fear wrestles with faith. I know theologically that God is in control, almighty in power, always near, and perfect in wisdom, love, and grace, but I don't always live like I actually believe these things are true. Sometimes I have a bit of the spirit of Jonah in me. You remember that God called Jonah to go and preach to the city of Nineveh, but Jonah ran as far as he could in the other direction. The boat he took to make his escape was caught in a storm (sent by God), and the sailors on the boat tried to figure out why. They found Jonah asleep in the bottom of the boat, and asked him who he was. Jonah replied, "I am a Hebrew, and I fear the LORD, the God of heaven, who made the sea and the dry land" (Jonah 1:9). Jonah said that he feared the Lord, but his actions in the face of God's call didn't look like the actions of a man whose heart was shaped by a deep reverential fear of the Lord at all. All of us are like Jonah at times; what we say we believe doesn't seem to shape the way we live.

Three things still live inside of us that tend to get in the way of a life of faith, that is, a life that is shaped by what the Bible has to say about who God is, what his will for us is, and what he has provided for us in the grace of his Son. Fear, complaint, and independence are all obstacles to a willing, joyful, faithful, and restful life of faith. The regular gathering of the church for worship and instruction has been designed by God to be one of his most valuable weapons in our fight against these.

Fear. Because we live in a fallen world that does not function as God intended and because evil was unleashed on the world in that horrible moment in the garden of Eden, we have legitimate reasons to fear. The sufferings of life in this fallen world will enter your door. Bad things will happen. So fear is not always wrong. In fact, there is a kind of fear that is the only thing that has the power to disarm all other fear. This kind of fear is not a paralyzing, anxiety-producing dread, but rather a reverential awe and willing submission that gives your heart a remarkable peace and calm. The fear I'm talking about is fear of God. When you have this kind of fear, you are so blown away by the glorious glory of God, his almighty power, his infinite wisdom, his boundless love, and his inextinguishable grace that all other fears are unable to capture and control the thoughts and desires of your heart. A biblical knowledge of God, his character, his will, and his plan can break your bondage to all other forms of fear.

We therefore need the gathering of the community of faith for worship and instruction because it is so easy to become God-forgetful. I wish I could say that I look at everything through the lens of the presence and glory of God, but I don't. I still have moments when I fall into God amnesia, when I don't have my God-glasses on. And when I do this, life in this fallen world looks impossibly fearful. Very often my fear is really God-forgetfulness. I need—again and again, by spoken word and worship—to have the eyes of my heart filled with the glory of my glorious Savior, Lord, friend, and King. I need this so that what I crave, what I think, what I decide, what I say, and what I do are shaped by the fear of rest and not the fear of dread. I love the gathering of the church for corporate worship because I need again and again to be awakened out of my God-forgetfulness, and I'm sure you need this too.

Complaint. Sin is self-centered. It is about what I want, when I want it, who I want to deliver it, and how I want it to de delivered. Sin places in me a desire to rule the world so that it does my bidding, and it causes my heart to be a personal pleasure center rather than a worship center. Therefore, complaint becomes more natural than thankfulness. Sin makes me reduce the field of my focus and concern down to my wants, my needs, and my feelings. Grace gives us eyes to see and hearts to love a greater glory than our own. It is God's grace alone that has the power to break our worship of ourselves and gives us hearts that worship and serve the one who made and sustains us. But as long as sin, with its self-orientation, still lives in us, our hearts will be pulled between gratitude and complaint. I wonder how many of us would have to admit that it is much easier on any given day to find more reason to complain than to praise. Would those who live with us or near us say that we are grateful? How often do we wonder where God is and what he is doing? How often are our hearts focused on what we don't have rather than on the lavish gifts of grace that have been poured down on us from our Father in heaven? Are we quicker to grumble than to give thanks?

I need to be reminded again and again of who I am and what I have been given, not because I have earned or deserve these gifts, but because of the loving and lavish generosity of the King of kings and Lord of lords, who by grace is my Father. Perhaps you've experienced your heart come to life in a worship service or in the middle of a sermon. I know I have. Maybe you have left a corporate worship service with an entirely different set of emotions than you came into the room with. I know I have. Maybe in the middle of a great hymn or worship song, you've been convicted that you tend to complain more at God than offer the gratitude of your heart to him. I know I have. Corporate worship is designed to give us eyes to see the myriad blessings that are ours as children of God, so that our lives would be shaped by worship and not complaint.

Independence. The greatest lie ever told was spoken by the serpent in the garden, when he proposed to Eve and Adam that it was possible for them to live independently. The worst decision ever made was when Adam and Eve decided to step away from dependence on and submission to God, thinking that they could somehow, some way be like him. Sin is fiercely independent. It is about self-rule. Sin hates authority. The life of sin is built on the delusion of independence. It buys into the fantasy that we are smart enough, powerful enough, and righteous enough to live on our own. As long as sin still lives in us, independence will war with submission to God in our hearts. That's why we don't really like being told what to do and why we chafe against little laws (think traffic or parking) in our lives. Parents, this is why your children debate you when told what they can eat, when they have to go to bed, or what they can watch on Netflix. They aren't just resisting the issue at hand; they are fighting authority. Sin reduces all of us to little self-sovereigns, loving rule more than loving being ruled.

So we all need to be reminded of the humbling truth that we are not wise enough, strong enough, or righteous enough to live on our own. We need the narrative of creation-fall-redemption, which is the overarching theme of Scripture, to confront us with the disaster of human independence and the danger it places us in if we give it room in our hearts. We need to be reminded that we find in God and God alone what we will never find in ourselves. He is the wisdom we need. He is the power we need. He is the righteousness we need. Life, in its eternal fullness, is only ever found in a willing submission of your heart and life to him. Grace doesn't lead us from dependence to independence, but rather from independence to a deeper and deeper dependence on God.

This week in the gathering of God's people, be glad that the artifacts of fear, complaint, and independence that still live in your heart will be exposed, and you will be lovingly welcomed once again to the best life ever, one that is lived in a practical, street-level, heartfelt dependence upon and submission to God.

———

Scripture: Isaiah 41:10 (fear), Philippians 2:14–15 (complaint), and Proverbs 3:5–6 (independence)

Reflections: In which of the obstacles to a joyful life of faith (fear, complaint, or independence) do your actions and thoughts not reflect what you say you believe? What could prompt you to remember to be trusting, thankful, and submissive to God?

Family Discussion: Ask members of the family to choose one of the above obstacles, and challenge them to memorize all or part of the corresponding Scripture passage, depending on age and ability. Discuss how God's word through corporate worship reminds us to trust him, practice thankfulness, and depend on him.

Sunday 5

Corporate worship is designed to define for you,
explain to you, and celebrate with you the wonder
of the grace of your eternal union with Christ.

ONE OF THE MOST BEAUTIFUL, heart-changing, and life-giving truths of the gospel is the truth of our union with Christ. When you hear "union with Christ," do you understand what it means? Do the glory of those words fill your heart? Does the thought of your union with Christ give you reason to get up in the morning, even when life is hard? Does it make you never tire of singing and celebrating God's grace with your brothers and sisters in the faith? Do you know what your union with Christ has to do with who you are and what you do every day? Do you grasp how it is meant to infuse you with help and hope? Do you know how it is meant to produce in you a heart of humble, unshakable gratitude right here, right now? Do you live in the peace and rest of what it means to be united to Christ by faith?

There is a reason union with Christ is such an important truth to understand and live in light of. Human beings made in the image of God live life based not on the *facts* of their existence but rather on their *interpretation* of the facts. God designed us to be meaning-makers. This capacity was given to us so that we could know God, know ourselves, and understand God's revelation of himself and his will for our lives. One of the most important aspects of this meaning-making function is our grappling with the question of who we are. Somehow, someway we are always assigning to ourselves some kind of identity. *Who am I?* The way you answer this profound question will shape the way you live your life. So it is vital for you to know that you have not just been forgiven by God and accepted into his family, but by grace you have been united to Christ. Your "in Christ" identity changes everything about your understanding of who you are and what your hope and potential are as a child of God. Understanding your union with Christ will change the way you think about and live in your marriage. It will alter your thoughts about your capability as a parent. It will change the way you approach your friendships, your life at your university, the way you think about your money and your sexuality, and a host of others things.

When it comes to the magnitude of the truth of our union with Christ, I think it is impossible for us to be taught about it too much, to be reminded of it too often, to sing about it too repeatedly, or to mediate upon it too deeply. The heart of the gathering of God's people should never be about what we are called to do for God, but it must always be about what he has done in his Son for us. The focus of this worship gathering is first on *being* and then on *doing*. And the center thought of what we are now as the children of God is our union with Christ. All of the gorgeous blessings of God's grace, which we examine and celebrate when we gather, flow out of the fact that by the power of God's grace, lost and foolish rebels have been united to Christ. Whether you understand it or not, your union with Christ changes everything for you. You have not just been forgiven; you have not just been accepted; you have not just been guaranteed a future. You are now living in the context of something that changes everything for your past, present, and future. You, believer, have been united to Christ. This reality and identity is more important than any other identity you could ever assign to yourself. Let me explain.

There is no better place to go to understand this union than Ephesians 1. Paul's passion for people to understand who they are and what they have been given in Christ is evident in verse after verse. As you read, pray that God would open your heart to the wonder of what we are about to consider:

Blessed be the God and Father of our Lord Jesus Christ, who has blessed us *in Christ* with every spiritual blessing in the heavenly places, even as he chose us *in him* before the foundation of the world, that we should be holy and blameless before him. In love he predestined us for adoption to himself as sons through Jesus Christ, according to the purpose of his will, to the praise of his glorious grace, with which he has blessed us in the Beloved. *In him* we have redemption through his blood, the forgiveness of our trespasses, according to the riches of his grace, which he lavished upon us, in all wisdom and insight making known to us the mystery of his will, according to his purpose, which he set forth *in Christ* as a plan for the fullness of time, to unite all things in him, things in heaven and things on earth.

In him we have obtained an inheritance, having been predestined according to the purpose of him who works all things according to the counsel of his will, so that we who were the first to hope *in Christ* might be to the praise of his glory. *In him* you also, when you heard the word of truth, the gospel of your salvation, and believed in him, were sealed with the promised Holy Spirit, who is the guarantee of our inheritance until we acquire possession of it, to the praise of his glory. (Eph. 1:3–14)

You could spend months meditating on the magnitude of what this passages says about who you are and what you have been given as a child of God. For now, let's focus on what Paul wants you to understand about what it means to be "in Christ."

Every spiritual blessing. Everything you need in order to live as God has called you to live, in every situation and relationship of your daily life, with every grace you need to do so, along with the guarantee of a glorious future without sin or suffering, are yours because you are in Christ.

He chose us in him before the foundation of the world. Before the world began God set his love on you and chose you to be the recipient of his justifying, sanctifying, and glorifying grace, so that you can stand before him holy and blameless. Because you are in Christ, you are not alone in your battle with sin. God's inexhaustible grace will keep doing its work until that work is complete.

In him we have the forgiveness of our trespasses, according to the riches of his grace. We no longer have to be paralyzed by sin's regret or defeated by sin's shame, because in Christ all of our sins—past, present, and future—have been forgiven, by means of his shed blood on the cross.

In him God has made known to us the mystery of his will. Our eyes were once blind and our hearts closed to the life-giving, life-changing wisdom of God's truth, but in Christ these mysteries have been opened and illumined to us. This is why our hearts respond to God's word.

In him we have obtained an inheritance. Peter says that this inheritance is being kept in heaven for us (1 Pet. 1:4). There is glory beyond our ability to conceive that awaits us, which we could have never earned or deserved, but which is ours in Christ.

In him we might live for the praise of his glory. In Christ we are blessed to live for a glory greater than our own, for a kingdom way better than our own, and for the praise of a King who is not us.

In him we were sealed with the promised Holy Spirit. This means that because you are in Christ, your relationship with God is never at risk, never at stake. Your relationship with God and your place in his eternal family have been sealed forever. Your continued obedience doesn't guarantee your standing with God; being in Christ does.

We often enter the public gathering of God's people having lived during the week in a state of "in Christ" amnesia. Sadly, our emotions, words, and actions have been negatively affected, because we have forgotten who we are and what has been lavished on us in Christ. So we need to hear again and again the amazing grace that is ours because we were chosen before the world began to be *in Christ*. This grace is not just a future reality; it provides everything we need to be what God has chosen us to be and to do what he has called us to do right here, right now. We simply can't gather enough, hear too often, or reflect too deeply on the warehouse of blessings that are ours in Christ.

———

Scripture: Romans 8:1–2

Reflections: From the above passage, reflect once more on how much you as a believer have to celebrate because you are *in Christ*.

Family Discussion: Ask family members to discuss one area of their lives or thoughts that should change because of their union with Christ (e.g., marriage, parenting, friendships, sexuality, etc.). Discuss the things that cause us to forget who we are and what has been lavished on us in Christ. What is the remedy for this *in Christ amnesia*?

Sunday 6

*Corporate worship is designed to help you take the eyes of
your heart off the difficulties of your situation and focus
them on the grace and glory of your ever-present Savior.*

I have an eyesight problem.
It's not that my physical eyes
are fading;
my problem is
the eyes of my heart.
I often lack
the clarity of vision,
the sightedness that is needed
to live as you intended,
to live with moral purpose,
to live with a submissive heart,
to live free of complaint,
to live gratefully,
to live with joy,
to live with a restful heart,

to live with confidence in you,
to live for a glory greater than my own,
to live with eternity in view,
to live with unshakable hope,
to live with humble courage,
to live a life shaped by love,
to live willing to forgive,
to live out of a generous heart,
to live grieved over my sin,
to live committed to confession and repentance,
to live resting in Christ's righteousness,
to live a life of faith and not fear,
to live believing you have given me everything I need,
to live free of idol worship,
to live with a tender, malleable heart,
to live—really live.
I too often let
struggles and disappointments of life
so dominate my vision,
my meditation,
my interpretations,
that I am temporarily blind
to you,
to your presence,
to your promises,
to your power,
to your ever-active grace.
When I do this,
I let trouble define me.

I let disappointments tell who I am.
I let the unwanted and unexpected
shape how I think about
my life and my potential.
I let fear overwhelm faith.
I let complaint replace praise.
I let my blindness cause me
to wonder where you are,
what you are doing,
if you hear my cries,
if your promises are still reliable.
I let my blindness cause me
to bring you into
the court of my judgment,
questioning your faithfulness and love.
So I run again with your people
to your temple,
not just to sing songs of redemption,
not just to hear your word's instruction,
but aided by these things
to open the eyes of my heart,
to gaze upon your beauty once again,
to have my vision corrected once again,
so that I once again see you
in the glory of your splendor,
in the majesty of your grace
and, having looked on your beauty,
to bow in joyful surrender
and to rise to live

with hope restored
and the courage of
faith renewed.

———

Scripture: Psalm 27:3–5

Reflections: Read the above Scripture passage and ponder how the psalmist can be so confident even in dire circumstances.

Family Discussion: Discuss why it is necessary to take our focus off of our circumstances and instead focus on our Savior. How difficult is this for each family member, and why?

Sunday 7

Corporate worship is designed to combine
knowledge of God with knowledge of self, so
we'll know who we are, what we all desperately
need, and who alone can provide it for us.

DURING MY YEARS OF sitting in a counseling office with people
who were dealing with situational, relational, or emotional difficulty
of some kind, two things struck me again and again. First, it was
quite regular that the people I was seeking to help had distorted
views of themselves. I don't mean that they were intentionally
crafting a false persona, but that they didn't know themselves as
well as they thought they did. A primary part of my work with
them was to bring them to a higher, much more accurate self-
knowledge. Since we all are in a process of God's work of personal
change, self-knowledge is essential. All of us need God's work of
personal transformation, but it's hard to be committed to change
if you are unable to see where change is needed. If you have an
inaccurate view of yourself and someone points out to you a place
where change is needed, you will be offended and resistant, even

though that person may have a more accurate view of you than you do. Inaccurate self-knowledge will keep you from benefiting from the sight-giving, change-producing ministry of the body of Christ that is one of God's good gifts to you.

A second thing concerned me even more deeply. Many of the people I counseled had a less-than-accurate knowledge of God. Even though they professed to be Bible believers, they had developed a view of God that was formed more out of their interpretation of their experiences than from the pages of Scripture. It is always important to make sure that the Bible's theology interprets your experiences for you, rather than your experiences shaping your theology. None of my counselees had intentionally abandoned biblical doctrine for some other worldview, but experiential corruptions had altered their view of God and his truth. As I would listen to them describe God, what he was doing and why he was doing it, I would immediately understand why they struggled to trust him. As I listened, I would think, "If I thought this is who God was, I wouldn't trust him either." The God they described was not the gloriously wise and powerful God who offers us his boundless love, amazing grace, and mercies, form-fit for our moments of need. If you have begun to conclude that God is not good, then you will not go to him for help, because you never seek the help of someone whom you've concluded does not have your best interest in mind. The opposite is true as well. If you are fully persuaded that God is good, in every way and all of the time, then you will be able to follow him even when he leads you through things that are hard. You are able to follow him, because you are fully persuaded that he knows what is best and calls you to what is best, precisely because he is good.

God designed us to live our lives at the intersection of knowledge of God and knowledge of self. Inaccuracy on either side will produce a harvest of bad fruit in your life. It is vital for all of us to be willing to humbly admit that some inaccuracies in both our view of God and our view of ourselves remain. By grace we are all in God's school of knowing, and none of us have graduated yet. We all need a deeper, fuller, and more accurate view of God, one that produces a heart at rest and a joyful willingness to surrender our lives to him. Because we are growing to know him more, we will be more and more free of doubt and fear. Part of the curriculum in God's school of knowing trains us in self-knowledge. For this God has given us the perfectly accurate mirror of his word. We can look into his word and see ourselves as we truly are and, because we do, we seek the help from our Savior and his people that we actually need.

In a moment of crushing personal trouble, King David said,

One thing have I asked of the LORD,
    that will I seek after:
that I may dwell in the house of the LORD
    all the days of my life,
to gaze upon the beauty of the LORD. (Ps. 27:4)

All of us should want this as well. David understands that he will accurately understand the ugly things of life in this fallen world only when he looks at them through the lens of the stunning beauty of his Lord. When you see God accurately, you are overwhelmed with his beauty, and when you are overwhelmed with his beauty, you have an entirely different attitude toward and response to the hardships of life between the "already" and the "not yet."

So, again and again, we run to the "temple," not just because it is our duty to do so, but because we know we need to see God for who he truly is and, in seeing him, be able to see ourselves with humility and clarity. All of this should result in progressive surrender to this one of such beauty and a deeper and more joyful celebration of the generosity of his grace. God designed corporate worship to be vision-correcting, as our sin-weakened and blinded eyes are given gospel glasses once again. Because sin is deceitful and Satan is the ultimate deceiver, as we bump our way through this groaning world, we develop eye problems. We don't see God in the expanse of his glory and we don't see ourselves with our ongoing need for grace. Our vision problems then begin to shape the way we live. We question God's goodness and the reliability of his word, which makes it hard then to follow him by faith. Before long the joy of our salvation is gone, we no longer hunger for the nourishment of God's word as we once did, and we have less joy in the gathering of his people.

So we need to run, run, and run again to his "temple" and, through word and song, gaze upon our Lord's beauty once more, thankful that he has given us the gathering of his church to help us to truly see and, in seeing, to know him more fully and ourselves more accurately.

Scripture: Romans 10:2–3 and 2 Peter 1:2–4

Reflections: Have you ever thought of living life according to this statement: "God designed us to live our lives at the intersection of knowledge of God and knowledge of self"? What does this mean?

Family Discussion: Talk about what inaccuracies you each have in both your view of God and your view of yourself. Discuss how we can grow in our knowledge of God and see ourselves as we really are.

Sunday 8

Corporate worship is designed to remind you not to be captured by the things of this earth but to continue to seek the things that are above, and that there is grace upon grace for this struggle.

A HINDU PRIEST came into the inner sanctum of the temple, bowed before an idol of wood, then proceeded to wash it, dress it, and put a bowl of rice and fruit in front of it. It was shocking to watch. As I observed this ritual, I said to myself, "Can't he see, doesn't he know that this idol is nothing? It isn't alive; it cannot see or hear; it will not eat the food offered. It has no power to bless this dear man with anything. It is powerless, devoid of life." The priest's worship and service were tragically misplaced. What a heart-destroying religious delusion. How could he be this blind? This priest had done this day after day. Yet this wooden god had never once moved, never said, "Thank you," never tenderly touched this man, and never once answered his prayers. This god was not a god at all. It was nothing more than a well-carved piece of wood, but deep in the priest's heart it was so much more.

What happened next was even more shocking. I thought that the service and observance were over, but they weren't. I watched as the priest knelt first and then lay on his stomach, with arms outstretched before this wooden deity. It was a picture of complete surrender. When you are in this position, you have given up all of your defenses and are lying utterly vulnerable, in powerless adoration and surrender. As I watched, tears filled my eyes. The blindness and darkness of this moment overwhelmed me. The depth of the evil bondage of idolatry hit me as it never had before. I wanted to run over and yank this man off the floor, but I couldn't. I wanted to run out of the temple, but I couldn't. I wanted to separate myself from this idolatry, but I couldn't.

I have thought back on that day many times. I have come to understand that my Lord, in his sovereign love for me, planned that day for me. He wanted me to physically see and feel the pain, blindness, darkness, and delusion of idolatry. He wanted me to see its heart- and life-capturing irrationality. He wanted me to understand that in my sin I too am quite capable of assigning power to people, physical things, experiences, and locations that they do not have. God had me in that room so that overt religious idolatry would expose the covert idols that so easily capture my heart, control my desires, and then shape my living. That moment in that temple in North India robbed me of the pride I carried around because I thought I had never been tempted by overt religious idols. I would never bow before images made from wood, metal, or stone. I know better than that. But I left the temple thinking, "Do I? Could it be that I share the priest's delusion? Could it be that there are places in my life where I ask created things to do what only the Creator can do? Could it be that I too look for life where it cannot be found? If I want to yank that priest off the floor, shouldn't I want to search for and, by grace, destroy all the subtle, covert nonreligious idols in my life that I bow in surrender to?"

One form of idolatry is infinitely more dangerous than the worship of formal, physical idols. This form of idolatry should offend and activate us more than the religious idols we might see and react to in our travels. Because of the tragedy that occurred in the garden of Eden, idolatry is not just a religious delusion; it is in fact a human condition. It is this human condition, of which we all are a part, that should trouble us more than formal religious idolatry ever does.

What is this form of idolatry I am talking about? It is idolatry of the heart (see Ezek. 14:4–5). It is every sinner's capacity to ask creation to do what only the Creator can do. It is looking horizontally for a savior. It is hoping that my job, my marriage, my children, my possessions, my power and control, my experiences and successes, my food, my knowledge, my physical strength and health, my appearance, and so on will give me satisfaction and freedom, healing, wholeness, and peace of heart. It is somehow, someway buying into the delusion that abundant life can be found outside of the person and work of the Lord Jesus Christ. It is surrendering the rulership of my heart to something other than the God who made me and who alone has rightful claim to the surrender of everything I am and have.

Idolatry is not just allowing yourself to be ruled by what is bad. No, good things can also function as god-replacements. *A desire for a good thing becomes a bad thing when it becomes a ruling thing.* For instance, it is good to desire wisdom and to want to be right, but you can't live or work with a person whose heart is controlled by the need to always be right. It is good to want to have some control in your life, but to live for control will harm you and those around you. I've seen pastors become absentee husbands and fathers out of the pursuit of ministry success.

Heart idolatry is so much more dangerous than religious idolatry because not only can you be an idolater while priding yourself that you're not, but more importantly whatever controls your heart will control your thoughts, desires, and choices and, therefore, the direction of your life. You can religiously "worship" God while your heart is controlled by other gods. So we need again and again to have our hearts confronted by, redirected by, and comforted by the presence and grace of the one true Messiah. We need to be reminded again and again to focus the eyes of our hearts on things above and not on the things of this earth. So we joyfully gather over and over again to remember and celebrate the glory and grace of the one who alone is able to give us life and, in so doing, can rescue us from all the false gods that battle for control of our hearts. We gather together to be confronted by and to confess our idolatry, so that we will know the freedom of worshiping God alone.

———

Scripture: Colossians 3:1–3

Reflections: Try to think of at least one place in your life where you ask created things to do what only the Creator can do. How can those idols of the heart be exposed for what they really are, and then be destroyed?

Family Discussion: Discuss why heart idolatry is so dangerous. How is it possible to know the freedom of worshiping God alone?

Sunday 9

*Corporate worship is designed to progressively
silence your grumbling and complaining and
replace them with gratitude and worship.*

"Why is this my job?"

"There's nothing to eat."

"Why are there always more bills than money to pay them?"

"I just can't relate to his preaching."

"I wish I owned a better house."

"Why do I always have to live near noisy neighbors?"

"Why are all the good foods unhealthy?"

"My kids are making me insane."

"There is never enough time in the day."

"This traffic drives me crazy."

"I wish my husband were more romantic."

"Why doesn't God answer my prayers?"

"I'm tired of being tired."

"My parents don't have a clue."

"If I were in charge, I would _____.

I am convinced that the universal language of a fallen world is grumbling. No matter who we are, no matter where we are, and no matter what is going on, we can always find a reason to grumble about something. Complaint, for most of us, is more natural than gratitude. Dissatisfaction is more natural than contentment. Want is more natural than worship. Numbering our complaints is more natural than counting our blessings. Focusing on what we don't have seems more natural than thinking about all that we have been given.

But our problem is deeper than the fact that we meditate on the wrong things. If, because of God's goodness, we have expansive reasons for praise but find ourselves too often complaining, wouldn't it make sense to wonder why? You might assume that I'm going to say we complain because sin is still inside of us. Well, that is an answer, but it's not enough of an answer. True, if Adam and Eve could not and would not be satisfied with life as God planned in a perfect world and wanted more, then no wonder in a fallen world, with sin now living inside of us, we complain so much. But this is not a specific enough answer.

Let's consider what sin does to us and how the regular gathering of the community of faith for worship is meant to help us in this struggle. The apostle Paul tells us in 2 Corinthians 5:15 that Jesus came so that those who live would no longer live for themselves. Jesus came to live a perfectly righteous life, to die an acceptable and substitutionary death, and to rise again, victorious over sin and death, so that we would be freed from our bondage to ourselves. Sin causes us to live for nothing greater than ourselves. Sin makes self-satisfaction the highest human purpose. The DNA of sin really is selfishness in the truest, deepest sense. Sin causes me to be too focused on what I want, too obsessed with what I need, and too cognizant all the time of how I feel. Sin causes me to migrate to the center of my world and to somehow, someway fall into thinking that life is all about me. So, then, it makes sense that I would have a "me-istic" way of looking at, understanding, and experiencing everything. I evaluate everything in my life according to whether it is good for *me* or bad for *me*.

But I was not designed to live this way. This me-istic way of living is never a recipe for happiness and contentment. It will always result in the pain of discontent, a life of disappointment, and a lifestyle of constant complaint. Let me put it this way. If you are in the center of your world and if what is most important to you is what you want, what you think you need, and how you are feeling, then there will be no end to the things you find to complain about. Why is this so? It's because you live in a fallen world that doesn't function the way God originally intended. It's because you are not sovereign and the world will not do your bidding. It's because God didn't design life between the "already" and the "not yet" to be comfortable; he designed it to be transformational. It's because God is calling you away from an allegiance to your way to a joyful surrender to his way. It's because God is taking you through things that you would have never chosen in order to produce in you things that you could have never achieved on your own.

When you are in the center of your world, you will always find things to complain about. Yes, it is true that Jesus came to break your bondage to you, but it is also true that as long as sin lives inside of us, artifacts of the old me-ism remain. You can be a child of God but still live for yourself in the situations and relationships of everyday life. A life of consistent complaint reveals who we are truly living for at street level.

So we gather again to worship because we need to be confronted again and again with the centrality of God in all things. We need to be reminded once again that everything in life is about him. We need to be called back once again to the mentality of Romans 11:36: "For from him and through him and to him are all things. To him be glory forever. Amen." We need our hearts and minds filled once again with the glory of his glory and the goodness of his grace. We need to see again that every good gift comes from him. We need to be told again and again that serving ourselves is bondage, but serving him is where freedom can be found. We need to see again the amazing blessings he has lavished on us, which we could never have earned or deserved. We need to understand again that he knows what we need far better than we ever will, and that what he wants for us is better than anything we could ever want for ourselves. And we need to leave corporate worship with hearts filled to overflowing with his blessings, carrying with us once more a commitment to be better at counting our blessings than we are at numbering our complaints.

Scripture: James 1:17

Reflections: In what types of situations do you find yourself complaining? In what ways have you put yourself at the center of your world when you see this happening?

Family Discussion: Talk about how you can encourage each other to have hearts of gratitude, when it seems more natural to complain.

Sunday 10

*Corporate worship is designed to deepen your
love for the giver so you will be progressively
free from worshiping the gift.*

A VERY RICH MAN once invited me to dinner at a lovely restaurant
with gorgeous food. I knew he wanted to talk to me about something, but most of the meal was occupied with casual conversation.
Finally he said, "I don't have many people I can talk to about the
burdens of wealth. Most people think that if you have as much
money as I have, you shouldn't have many burdens, but that's
not true." He went on to say, "One of the biggest burdens for me
is that, because I am rich, I don't know who my real friends are.
I don't know if people want to be around me because they like me
and care about me or because they think I can do things for them.
I live wondering all the time if people want me or if they just want
my wallet. Often I am surrounded by people, but feel sort of alone.
I'm afraid they are hanging around not for what we can mutually
give each other as friends, but for what they can get from me. I'm
afraid people don't really see me, but that they see only my money."

I have thought about that conversation many times and wondered, "Is this what I do with the richest (in every way) person I know, the King of kings and Lord of lords?" It is tempting for us to love the lavish things the giver so generously blesses us with more than we love him. When we do this, we turn God into a vending machine. We put in a couple of prayer coins and press the "amen" button with the expectation that God will give us what we have set our hearts on. In this way prayer, which seems to be our most direct Godward act, can actually be idolatrous. If the thing that draws us into prayer is not a love for God and a surrender to his will ("your kingdom come, your will be done"), but rather is dominated by requests for the delivery of things that have captured our hearts, then what seems like an act of worship of the Creator is really an act of worshiping the creation.

If you love the giver, then you love his will, you prize his commands, you seek his glory, and you trust that he will meet your needs. If you love the giver, you want him to be pleased by how you live, so you are quick to confess your sin and rest in his forgiveness. If you love the giver, then you surrender your allegiance to your little kingdom of one and give yourself to the greater purposes of his kingdom. If you love the giver, you love his family, the church, and give yourself to its life, health, and mission. If you love the giver, you don't demand that he serve you, but you make sacrifices in service of him. If you love the giver, you love the gatherings of his people where, in words and song, you publicly express that love and focus your attention on the instruction he has lovingly left for you in his word. If you love the giver, your life is not shaped and directed by "I want" but by "God wants."

I don't know about you, but I spend so much of my time focusing on the creation (people, places, and things), so much of my time thinking about the duties and responsibilities of the day, and so much of my time meeting my own needs, that I need a regularly scheduled time when, along with others, I focus on the glorious glory of my Lord. I need to remember that he is perfect all of the time and in every way. I need to be reminded that he is the final definition of love. I need to see once again that all of his ways are right and true. I need to be confronted once more with the truth that he knows more about what I truly need than I ever will. And I need to be comforted with the stunning reality that this God of such perfection and beauty is now my Father by grace.

> One thing have I asked of the LORD,
>   that will I seek after:
> that I may dwell in the house of the LORD
>   all the days of my life,
> to gaze upon the beauty of the LORD
>   and to inquire in his temple. (Ps. 27:4)

I need the regular gathering of the church so I can get my awe back. I need to stand in silent, weak-kneed, slack-jawed, and heart-focused wonder before him once again as I hear his glory sung into my ears and preached into my heart. It is important that he loom before me with such beauty that it redefines the way I understand and experience every hard thing in my life. And I need to be filled with such a vibrantly alive love for him that there is no room for my heart to be captured and controlled by the love of something or someone else.

It's important to understand that love is spiritual warfare. Think of marital love. From the very first moment of commitment, your love is assaulted by challenges and temptations.

Passivity in marriage never produces anything good. From the earliest moments of commitment you have to fight for your love. You can forget your early adoration of your spouse. You can forget how differences in culture and personality attracted you rather than irritated you. Your eyes may wander to other potential lovers or your mind may wonder what it would have been like to marry someone else. If you really love your spouse, you do things to fight for your love, to revive it, to enhance it, and to deepen it.

So it is with your love of the Lord. It will be assaulted by the difficulties of life in this fallen world. It will be challenged as God brings things into your life that you didn't expect or don't want. It will be threatened by your wandering heart, which is not yet free from chasing after God replacements. Your love for God will suffer from seasons of inattention. But you cannot spiritually coast. Between the "already" and the "not yet" your love for the giver is under threat. Because you know this, you must be thankful for the gathering of God's people because here again and again you will be reminded that no gift will ever be as wonderful as the giver and that the giver is, himself, the best gift you have ever been given.

———

Scripture: Psalm 42:1–2

Reflections: When was the last time you were in awe of God's glory? How can you grow in your awe of God in the everyday of life?

Family Discussion: Discuss what it means to *spiritually coast* and how we can avoid doing this amid the busyness of life.

Sunday 11

Corporate worship is designed to produce sadness
(because of sin and brokenness) and celebration
(because of salvation and redemption).

NO ONE LIKES BAD NEWS. We spend a lot of mental and emotional time hoping for good news, but sometimes bad news is exactly what we need.

I recall sitting in the emergency waiting room with Luella, waiting and hoping for good news. I had been experiencing some minor symptoms, so I called my doctor. He reminded me that we live two blocks from a wonderful hospital and told me I should just go there and get things checked out. He seemed quite relaxed about my physical condition, so I was too. Luella and I sat calmly and occupied our time in the emergency waiting room watching the Philadelphia Eagles. After the typically long wait, I was called back into an examining room. I had good news on my mind. I thought they would check me out and send me home. That week I had done my ten-mile morning sprints on my bike and, other than my seemingly minor symptoms, I felt fine.

I did not get the good news I expected. I got very bad news. Heads of various departments in the hospital gathered in my examining room. I was disheartened and confused. Before long I was subjected to painful procedures, because my condition was quite serious. I was told that I was not going home; in fact, I wouldn't go home for ten days. After I was taken up to my hospital room, I began to have full-body spasms. They were both terrifying and horribly painful. The next day a doctor told me that because of blockages, my kidneys were dying, which meant they would have to do everything they could to reverse that trend. In my hospital bed I began to absorb the news that I would never be truly healthy for the rest of my life.

That stay in the hospital was followed by six surgeries in two years. I have now had ten surgeries in seven years. I have experienced weakness like I never knew before. I am living with limits I never had before. Considering all that God had called and blessed me to do, this life of weakness made no sense to me. But I have come to understand that the bad news, which I wanted so much to deny, was necessary for me to accept and live in the hope of the good news that I desperately needed.

I am embarrassed to admit that much of what I thought was faith in Jesus Christ was actually self-reliance. I was healthy and strong, and I had the ability to produce a lot quickly. I was proud of my physical condition and my industrious busyness. I said yes quickly to opportunities, because I knew I could do them. I got up early and stayed up late and kept busy in between. I wasn't weak, and I liked that. I wasn't needy, and I was proud of it. But God had something better for me: the bad news of weakness. Don't misunderstand. My weakness wasn't a punishment; it was a gift of grace. In my weakness, I began to cry out for the help of my Lord in ways I had never cried out before. In my weakness, I became more thankful than ever for his tender care and the power of divine grace. In my weakness, I began to understand that God didn't call me because I was strong and capable and that, in fact, my delusions of strength kept me from seeking and celebrating him. That bad news of my health opened my heart to receive waves and waves of glorious gospel news. I wasn't left with bad news, but I needed the bad news to hear, receive, and live in the good news of the gospel in ways I had never done before. I can say without hesitation that if what it took for me to be spiritually where I am right now was this very bad news about my health, I would gladly receive this news again (James 1:2–4).

So it is with the gathering of the church for worship. God does not intend for worship to be a comfortable good-news party. It isn't meant to be a place where we feel good about ourselves and where our self-reliance is strengthened. Corporate worship isn't meant to be the place where we're promised the good life, free from difficulty and disappointment. Corporate worship isn't designed to be religious entertainment for the spiritually satisfied, with music and teaching designed to make us comfortable. Worship that is void of any bad news whatsoever robs us of our hunger for the truly good news of the gospel. That kind of worship destroys true, humble confession. If our confession includes minimizing, excusing, and shifting the blame for our sin, then it's not confession at all, but rather self-righteousness dressed up in a gospel costume.

Corporate worship is meant to confront us with devastating, humbling, and heartbreaking bad news: we have no ability on our own to escape the saddest and most destructive thing that has ever infected humanity, the disease of our sin. This disease is universal, unavoidable, and terminal apart from divine intervention. But the news is even worse than what I've described. It is possible to walk around quite sad about the existence of sin in the world, but be way more concerned about the sin of others than you are with your own sin. This is a morally dangerous place to be. So we need to hear the baddest of the bad news, that our biggest problem in all of life is *us*. We need to hear that our greatest moral danger lives not outside of us but inside of us, and that there is no way we can escape that danger on our own. This bad news, which we need to hear again and again, is meant to crush two things that keep us from seeking and celebrating God's amazing grace: self-righteousness and self-reliance. It's the sadness of sin that produces the celebration of grace. We need corporate worship so that we would live as sad celebrants—not denying our sin, yet not defeated by it—because acceptance of the bad news opens hearts to seek and celebrate the good news of forgiving, accepting, empowering, transforming, and delivering grace. Weeping over sin together produces a celebration that is like no other. So, as you gather this weekend, let the bad news confront you so the good news can comfort and claim your heart.

———

Scripture: Ephesians 2:1, 4–7

Reflections: Why is understanding our sin a necessary part of genuinely celebrating the gospel?

Family Discussion: Talk about a time when some bad news helped you to appreciate the good news in ways you hadn't before.

Sunday 12

Corporate worship is designed to remind us
that nothing in us or around us is hidden from
God's eyes, and that this is very good news.

MY GRANDDAUGHTERS are obsessed with hide-and-seek. When we are with them, we always end up playing it. The game unfolds the same way every time. They are not very good at hiding, and we are too good at finding. So we have to pretend that we can't find them and act like we're about ready to give up. They, on the other hand, always have trouble finding us, so just as they are about to give up, we begin whistling or clapping until they finally find us. For some reason my granddaughters love to hide and really love it when they think they've fooled us.

The first moment of human hiding was anything but a game. It was one of the saddest, most shocking moments in the biblical record. Adam and Eve were created to live in the most beautiful relationship anyone could ever have, a relationship with God. They were created to live in a worshipful, obedient, and loving relationship with their Creator. They were designed to live with him and before him out in the open, with nothing to regret or fear. God walked with them in the perfect garden that he had made for them. They were made for situational and relational bliss. But in this shocking moment we find them hiding from God. It's weird and unnatural. When we encounter Adam and Eve hiding in the garden, it's immediately clear that something has gone very wrong. Instead of longing to once again be with God, they are afraid to be seen by him. Sin had entered the world, and the guilt and fear of sin caused them to hide. People have been hiding from God ever since. John said it this way: "And this is the judgment: the light has come into the world, and people loved the darkness rather than the light because their works were evil" (John 3:19).

One of the most important functions of corporate worship is that it again and again exposes the destructive delusion of our hiding. It not only teaches us that hiding sin never goes anywhere good, but it also presents to us a God from whom we cannot hide. God, in his glorious glory, is omnipresent, all-seeing, and all-knowing. There is no place that he is not, there is nothing he doesn't see, and there is nothing he doesn't know, so any attempt to hide from him is an act of spiritual insanity. God designed corporate worship to rescue us from this insanity. It is the greatest comfort ever that we cannot escape his presence. By grace, God watches over us with the compassionate heart of a loving Father, protecting, providing, rescuing, and guiding. It is a good thing to be reminded again and again that we cannot hide from him.

It is a haunting and glorious thought:
nothing is hidden from you.
You see me
on the mountain peak,

in the lowest valley,
in the forest density,
slipping between urban towers,
sliding behind my desk,
walking alone,
lost in the throng,
opening the next door,
leaving something behind,
propelled across oceans,
once again at home,
pulling the covers over me,
sitting before a glowing screen,
huddled in quiet thought,
no location hidden,
no action unseen,
never lost in the crowd.
It often haunts me
that I am always exposed,
always under the unceasing watch
of your righteous eyes.
There is no hiding place,
no escape from your holy presence.
But your eye on me is also
my eternal comfort.
You look on me with the eyes of a Father,
always guiding,
always protecting,
always providing,
always preparing the way.
You see my burdens and my grieving.

You see my laughter and my rejoicing.
You see my doubt and my fearing.
You know my hopes and my dreaming.
You hear my praise and my weeping.
I know you see and care for me.
So, when I feel exposed by your
holy eyes,
I will remember that Jesus is my
righteousness,
and when I feel alone,
I will bask in the comfort of knowing
your eyes watch over me,
and in your watching, there is safety.

Corporate worship is an invitation to come out of hiding and to bask in the beauty of knowing and being known by God, a beauty that is ours because of his redeeming grace.

———

Scripture: Psalm 139:1–12

Reflections: Which verses are especially encouraging to you from the above passage?

Family Discussion: Is it a haunting or comforting thought that God's watchful eyes are always on you? Why?

Sunday 13

*Corporate worship is designed to stimulate you to make
sure your life today is shaped by the surety and glory of
what God has promised you on that final day yet to come.*

RICK WAS SO SHORTSIGHTED. He loved to work, and he loved
the fruits of his material success. There was no opportunity he
didn't jump on. As he took on more and more, his time away
from his wife and children increased. Each day he left the house
before any of his family had gotten up, and he came home when
most of them were in bed. He never saw his children and had
little time to invest in his relationship with his wife. The details
of his job captured his mind and controlled his activity. He was
the ultimate example of living for the moment; each moment of
opportunity, challenge, and success was more exciting than the
last. He worked as fast as he could and spent as fast as he worked.
He led an intoxicatingly shortsighted existence fueled by visions
of more and better. But shortsighted living seldom contributes
to long-term gain in the places that really count. Sadly, this man
ended up with a broken marriage and an estranged relationship

with his children. He constantly thought about success, but seldom thought about his legacy.

Emily was seventeen and about to graduate from high school. She was excited about what was to come. In the dizzying days of proms, final exams, and graduation parties, all kinds of commercial "congratulation graduate" offers came in the mail. The one that caught her attention was a preapproved credit card (something a seventeen-year-old should never have). She squealed as she open the envelope and said, "I can't believe it. I can finally get a car!" She looked at that card with a credit limit of ten thousand dollars and immediately thought, "I can get a decent car for that amount." What she wanted, but could not actually afford, seemed to her to now be possible. She did not consider how much that car would actually cost her, at an interest rate of 25 percent, or the fact that she would probably still be making payments on it long after the car was no longer usable. Shortsightedness is often about today's desires, and it seldom considers long-term plans or consequences. I have counseled many people in midlife who wished they could go back and relive their young adult years, because they were still dealing with the consequences in life and work of the shortsighted choices they made.

Here is where the gospel of Jesus Christ rescues us from us. The gospel narrative pushes us to live with eternity in view. It calls us away from focusing only on the pleasures, the opportunities, the temptations, the responsibilities, and the cravings of this moment. In fact, the gospel teaches us that we will never understand what is happening in the present unless we look at it in light of eternity. It calls us away from living for what we can grab *now* and to a life that is formed by what God has promised us *then*. Here, too, is where the gathering of the community of faith is so vital. I am very aware that I can fall into living like an eternity amnesiac. Whatever is going on in the moment so captures my thoughts and desires that I lose my gospel mind. I lose a sense of who I am by grace, and I lose sight of the glory of what God had promised me.

Our Lord knew how shortsighted and distractable we would be. He knew that no matter how correct our theology of eternity was, there would be moments in our everyday lives where we would forget what is to come and live as if this moment were all we had. So our Lord designed the corporate gathering of his people for us. It is his gift for our rescue, guidance, and protection. As we gather, we are reminded once again that by grace our little stories have been embedded in the eternal story of redemption. In worship we are called again and again to live not with a "my story" mentality but with a "God's story" mentality. By song and word we are reminded of the glory that awaits us, and we are called to live with eternity in view. As we gather with the weight and concerns of life in this fallen world, we are comforted with the truth that because we are the children of God, now is not all we have. No, we have a destiny coming where all the weighty and hurtful things that get us down will be no more, and we will live forever in a place where peace and righteousness reign forever and ever.

Remembering our promised and guaranteed destiny serves us in a variety of ways. First, as Scripture enables us to listen to the voices of those now on the other side, we are able to have our values clarified. The saints who are now before God's throne do not celebrate big houses, material success, or personal power. No, they celebrate the one who faithfully did in them, for them, and through them everything he promised. The most practically valuable thing to them now is their redemption, and what captures their hearts more than anything else is their Redeemer.

And we are invited to listen to and learn from them, so that we would live by those same values now. Living with eternity in view means that the life-shaping love that has captured and controls my heart is love for my Lord and, because it is, I follow him with willingness and joy.

Living with God's promise of the destiny to come in view is also an important tool for having peace in hardship, disappointment, and suffering. When you are in the middle of devastating hardship, it feels as if that hardship is ultimate. It feels as if you are in the defining moment of your existence. But hardship is not ultimate; God is. Hardship does not define you; God's promise does. When viewed from the perspective of the unending years of eternity, my current suffering is a flash of a moment. The Bible never minimizes or denies what we suffer, but the hugeness of the promise of God's plan gives us comforting perspective on what we suffer. This is why Paul is able to call our present moments of suffering "light and momentary" (2 Cor. 4:17). Our suffering will end, and we will forever live in a kingdom where no one will ever suffer in any way again.

The promise of the glorious destiny to come also quiets our fears and anxieties. It reminds us that our lives are not out of control. Yes, they are frequently out of *our* control, but not our Lord's. He is in control of every aspect of our present and our future, and no matter how things might appear to us right now, he is marching us toward a glory beyond our wildest imaginations.

So we gather to have the comfort and motivation of our eternal destiny focused and stimulated once again. We gather once again to remember that we will live properly now only when we live in light of then. And we gather to remember that we are blessed that grace has placed us in the hands of one who loves us enough to make such glorious promises and who has the willingness and power to deliver them.

———

Scripture: 2 Corinthians 4:18 and Hebrews 12:1–2

Reflections: What are the things that dull your awareness of eternal glory? Are you ever tempted to live as if this present moment is the only thing that matters?

Family Discussion: Consider the ways in which the gospel of Jesus Christ rescues us from us.

Sunday 14

*Corporate worship is designed to instill in you a
deeper confidence in your Savior and the power
of his ever-present, inexhaustible grace.*

I HAVE SOME QUESTIONS FOR YOU. Don't answer quickly. Take
time to examine yourself in light of each question.

Are you confident?
Does fear capture you?
Does anxiety haunt you?
Does regret paralyze you?
Does envy cause you to be a bit bitter?
Does doubt rob you of your joy and motivation?
Do you live a life of courage or timidity?
Do you wonder if God loves you?
Do you struggle to believe that his promises are true?
Do you hold your beliefs with confidence?
Do you wonder whether God is really in control?
Do you question why a good God would rule his world in the
way he does?

Do you struggle to follow God's clear commands?
Do you rest in God's wisdom?
Is your life shaped by hope?
Is your life shaped more by fear or by faith?
Is God in your final thoughts before you go to bed at night and your first thought when you get up in the morning?

Moments of doubt are a normal part of the life of faith. My honest confession is that many doubts have arisen along my spiritual pathway. God's word is clear, but his sovereign rule isn't always clear to us. We all have times when we wonder what God is doing, why he has brought certain things into our lives, or why he is ruling the world in the way he is. This confusion is pictured for us in the Psalms. Below is a brief selection.

> How long, O LORD? Will you forget me forever?
>   How long will you hide your face from me?
> How long must I take counsel in my soul
>   and have sorrow in my heart all the day?
> How long shall my enemy be exalted over me?
>   (Ps. 13:1–2)

> I say to God, my rock:
>   "Why have you forgotten me?
> Why do I go mourning
>   because of the oppression of the enemy?"
> As with a deadly wound in my bones,
>   my adversaries taunt me,
> while they say to me all the day long,
>   "Where is your God?" (Ps. 42:9–10)

For you are the God in whom I take refuge;
    why have you rejected me?
Why do I go about mourning
    because of the oppression of the enemy? (Ps. 43:2)

Behold, these are the wicked;
    always at ease, they increase in riches.
All in vain have I kept my heart clean
    and washed my hands in innocence.
For all the day long I have been stricken
    and rebuked every morning. (Ps. 73:12–14)

O God, why do you cast us off forever?
    Why does your anger smoke against the sheep of your
        pasture? (Ps. 74:1)

I am shut in so that I cannot escape;
    my eye grows dim through sorrow.
Every day I call upon you, O LORD;
    I spread out my hands to you.
Do you work wonders for the dead?
    Do the departed rise up to praise you? (Ps. 88:8–10)

Again and again the Psalms picture the confusion of God's children as they seek to understand the purposes of God. We, along with them, are often left wondering and confused, because God has not opened the doors to his secret will to us, nor has he called us to try to figure these mysteries out. God's secret will is called his secret will because it is secret. I have the clear wisdom and guidance of his word to guide me in my everyday living, but

I still go through moments of anguish when God seems distant and unhearing or when what he is doing does not seem loving or good. It is important to understand and admit that, this side of eternity, doubt will enter your mind.

We must distinguish between the doubt of *wonderment* and the doubt of *judgment*. The doubt of wonderment is a normal confusion every believer will face, because God's thoughts are not like our thoughts and his ways are not like ours. Sometimes what God sees as wise and good will look like neither to us. In the grandeur of his infinite wisdom, God will leave us wondering. So, in our wonderment, we run to God for help and rest. This is what these psalms depict. They are cries for help in the midst of the pain of confusion. In our wonderment we run to his word for clarity and comfort. In our wonderment we run to his people for counsel and encouragement. We run to the gathering of his children, so that progressively our rest and confidence in our Savior grows and deepens.

The doubt of judgment is when your wonderment has morphed into vertical judgment. You conclude that God is not good and therefore not worthy of your trust. You somehow, someway, and for some reason have brought God into your court of judgment and sentenced him as being less than what he has declared himself to be. When you have made this conclusion, you no longer have confidence in the truthfulness of his word or a desire to gather with his people.

So we gather again and again for instruction and encouragement. We gather so that the glory and grace of the Lord looms large in our hearts. We gather so that our seasons of wonderment will never morph into vertical judgment, where we become comfortable with no longer entrusting ourselves to the Lord.

———

Scripture: Romans 11:33–36

Reflections: Have you ever felt the pain of confusion about what God is doing as depicted in the above psalms? How do you keep from slipping into judging God in these situations?

Family Discussion: Discuss how the psalms and Romans 11:33–36 can be an encouragement in times of doubt.

Sunday 15

*Corporate worship is designed to remind us that the
incarnation of Jesus Christ defines what all of us need and
points us to the only one who will ever meet that need.*

I WAS REBUKED, and it stung. As my colleague confronted me,
I felt my chest tighten and my ears get warm. I wanted to rise to
my defense, to tell him that he misunderstood what I had done.
I wanted to let him know that I wasn't the only sinner in the room;
I'd known him long enough to see his weaknesses and failures too.
I wanted to be self-righteously angry, but I couldn't. I knew he was
right. I knew he saw me in a particular situation with greater accuracy than I saw myself. It was an awkward and tense moment, but
in the tension I felt the heart-piercing pain of the convicting grace
of the Holy Spirit. My need to defend myself to my friend melted
away and began to be replaced by humble grief and a desire to own
the substance of his rebuke and confess my sin. As I responded to
God, the tension was broken. Defensiveness gave way to gratitude
for both God and my friend. I walked away with a burden lifted
and a relationship reconciled.

I don't know anyone who likes rebuke. None of us have ever thought, "I just wish I could be rebuked more." Rebuke often carries connotations of condemnation in our thinking, as we imagine a pointed finger, raised volume, inflammatory language, and judgment. But God's rebuke is not like that. It is not a precursor to judgment but rather an act of redeeming love. God's rebuke is never about giving up on us; it's about investing in us once again. God rebukes us because we need it. In the blindness of sin, we often think we are way more righteous than we actually are and way more faithful than we really have been. We all have the ability to name our sin as something less than sin or to compare ourselves to other sinners and conclude that we are not so bad after all. We are all good at rewriting our history in ways that shift blame away from us onto something or someone else. No matter how long we have followed our Savior, we all continue to need the grace of his loving rebuke. You could say it this way: whom the Lord loves, he rebukes. As Hebrews 3:12 tells us, "Take care, brothers, lest there be in any of you an evil, unbelieving heart, leading you to fall away from the living God."

We find one particularly stunning, world-changing moment of rebuke in Scripture. You could argue that this moment, in God's sovereign and redeeming plan, is the rebuke of rebukes. You want to make sure you don't miss it. The incarnation of Jesus, that is, the invasion by grace of the Son of God into the world he created, but which is now fallen, is the most pointed and significant moment of confrontation that has ever or will ever happen. The birth of Jesus confronts each of us with the fact that sin is real and inescapable, and it leads to death. In his coming we are forced to face the humbling fact that the greatest danger to all of us exists inside of us and not outside of us. The birth of Jesus requires us to confess that we are not okay and our world is not okay. The coming of Jesus yanks us out of our spiritual complacency to see that our spiritual condition really is a matter of life and death. It is in the birth of Jesus that pride in our own wisdom, strength, and righteousness is revealed for what it is: an eternally dangerous spiritual delusion. Only in the radical intervention of the incarnation can we see ourselves with accuracy. We cannot be what we are supposed to be and do what we have been created to do independent of divine rescue. Jesus came because there is no other way for what sin has broken to be restored. If we were enough, if our righteousness were enough, if we were powerful enough, if we knew enough, and if we were spiritually healthy enough, then there would have been no reason for Jesus to come.

This is why is it is important for us to gather with one another again and again, in worship service after service, to focus again and again on one thing: the person and work of Jesus. It is vital for us to be reminded again and again that his primary mission was not to be our teacher, our healer, or our example. Yes, by grace, he is all of these things to us, but it is important to understand that he came to be our *Jesus*, that is, the one who would save us from the thing we could not save ourselves from: sin. Sin is the biggest of all human problems, and it lies at the heart of all other human tragedies. Before sin entered the world, there was no sadness, no sickness, no suffering of any kind. Everything was where it was meant to be and doing exactly what God designed it to do. Everything. Sin broke the cosmos in the deepest and most fundamental way. It left a world that is groaning and in need of redemption. Sin is at the root of life's hardships. Sin is the reason relationships can be so hurtful. Sin is the cause of personal, familial, and international war. Sin corrupts our motives, distorts our desires, and perverts our intentions. Every human being is disappointed in some way. Every human being longs for a better world. Every human being shops for some truth that will liberate them from the mess. Every human being follows some kind of messiah.

Every human being carries a contradiction. We all, in some way, recognize that there is evil in our world, that people can be cruel, and that institutions are often corrupt. We complain about what others do, we point the finger of blame quite often, and we mourn the corrupted power of institutions around us, but we want to believe that we are different. We want to think that we are one of the good guys. We point to sin external while we deny sin internal. But if there were no individual internal state of sin, then there would be no cruel people, no misused power, and no corrupt institutions. Yet we mourn the condition of the world as we minimize our own sin and work to convince ourselves that we are righteous. This is why we need the loving confrontation of the radical intervention of the incarnation to remind us that we are not okay. There is no way to explain the birth, life, death, and resurrection of Jesus if we are able to stand before God *without* a Messiah and be okay in his sight.

Jesus's birth is the ultimate diagnostic of the human condition. It is the moment in history that we should never stop considering. We are weak, broken, and in need of redemption. That is why the Savior came. So we gather and remember, lest in our delusion we forget who we really are, what we so deeply need, and what God alone has given us in the birth of his Son.

———

Scripture: Matthew 1:21

Reflections: What does the statement "Every human being follows some kind of messiah" mean?

Family Discussion: Discuss how the incarnation of Jesus Christ is the *rebuke of rebukes.*

Sunday 16

*Corporate worship is designed to draw you in to a
joyful intentionality of worship of your Sovereign
Lord Redeemer that doesn't end after the service but
shapes the way you live every day of the week.*

AT A RECENT parenting conference, I taught that the most significant issue in a child's life is worship. I could see the confusion
on the parents' faces. They were probably thinking, "I came to get
help with all of the hard stuff going on with my kids, things that
drive me crazy. I have no idea how to handle my kids, and he's up
there talking about worship. What does that have to do with my
son's refusal to eat what I prepare or my daughter's desire to wear
things that I think are inappropriate? What does worship have to
do with what I struggle with every day as a parent? I want practical
help. Please don't talk to me about worship!"

As I looked at the confused faces in the crowd, I was neither
surprised nor discouraged. I have seen that reaction countless
times, and it has convinced me that many of us have a spiritual
problem we don't even know we have. The parents were confused

when I said that the most important issue in their child's life was worship, because when they heard *worship*, they immediately thought of Sunday morning. Most of those parents had no bigger concept of worship than the formal, gathered religious worship service they attended each week. But the Bible's concept of worship is much broader, much deeper, and much more connected to daily life than that.

Note the words of Romans 1:25: "They exchanged the truth about God for a lie and worshiped and served the creature rather than the Creator, who is blessed forever! Amen." It is clear that the way Paul uses the word *worship* here is not as a formal religious concept. Then what is Paul talking about here? He is talking about something that happens in our daily lives. First, it is vital to understand that worship is much more than a religious activity. Worship in its most basic definition is about human identity. Every human being is a worshiper. This worship capacity was wired into every human being to drive him to his Creator. So every human being worships. The most irreverent, irreligious person worships. Paul doesn't divide people into those who worship and those who don't. No, Paul divides people by who or what they worship. And there are only two choices. You will worship your Creator, or you will worship something in creation.

We also must understand how the Bible uses the word *heart*. When the Bible talks about the heart, it is not talking about that blood pump in your chest. No, it is talking about the causal core of your personhood. As the center of your thoughts, desires, emotions, and will, the heart is your control center. Your heart determines what you choose, what you say, and how you act. The heart is the worship center of every human being. Every function of the heart is controlled by what the heart worships. Our hearts always function under the rule and the control of something. We either do what we do out of love for and service of the Creator or of some created thing. This means that every single thing in our lives is shaped by the worship of *something*.

Here's what is so important about this discussion. It is possible to have embraced a solidly biblical theology, to be quite biblically literate, and to be a regular participant in formal worship, and at the same time have idols in your heart that cause you to do and say things that are not consistent with what you have professed to believe. Ezekiel 14 points to this:

> Then certain of the elders of Israel came to me and sat before me. And the word of the LORD came to me: "Son of man, these men have taken their idols into their hearts, and set the stumbling block of their iniquity before their faces. Should I indeed let myself be consulted by them? Therefore speak to them and say to them, Thus says the Lord GOD: Any one of the house of Israel who takes his idols into his heart and sets the stumbling block of his iniquity before his face, and yet comes to the prophet, I the LORD will answer him as he comes with the multitude of his idols, that I may lay hold of the hearts of the house of Israel, who are all estranged from me through their idols. (Ezek. 14:1–5)

Picture the scene. The spiritual leadership of Israel come to the prophet to ask questions of the Lord. But the Lord recognizes that they have idols in their hearts, and when you have an idol in your heart, it puts moral stumbling blocks in your life. So God tells them that he will not answer their questions, because all he is interested in is their idols. God knows that if he gives advice to idolaters, they will use the advice to serve the idols that control their hearts.

God wants to "lay hold of our hearts," so he has designed the gathering of his church to expose our idolatry and to remind us once again that no created thing will ever be able to deliver the satisfaction, peace, hope, joy, and freedom that the Creator alone can give us. The regular gathering of the church is meant to remind us that we don't so much need behavioral management, but rather we need worship realignment. If your heart wanders away from worship and service of the Creator and gives itself to some God-replacement, then your thoughts and desires, choices and actions will wander away too. The purpose of the gathering of God's people is not just to be the place where we worship; it is also to be the place where our everyday worship is reclaimed and redirected, so that everything we do and say is an expression of hearts held by the Creator and lives shaped by a joyful surrender to him. We drag our idols into the gathering again and again. With each gathering, once again we are given eyes to see, so we can confess our disloyalty to our Creator. This allows us to leave gathered worship with a renewed commitment to put a hammer to the feet of our idols and bow in daily surrender to our Lord and King. Corporate worship is one of God's primary heart reclamation tools. Rather than punish us for our idolatry, he woos us back to himself over and over again and sends us out into the world with renewed loyalty to his plan, new motivation to live inside of the boundaries of his will for us, and a renewed commitment to live for his glory. What grace!

Scripture: Romans 12:1

Reflections: What are the idols in your heart that need to be exposed in order for your worship to be reclaimed and redirected?

Family Discussion: Discuss the importance of the statement, "Every human being is a worshiper." How will realizing this change our everyday lives?

Sunday 17

Corporate worship is designed to remind you that
everything in life will fail you. Build your hope in Jesus.

WHEN OUR FOUR CHILDREN were at home, we drove the classic family minivan. Ours had seen better days, but to my nonmechanical mind, it seemed to be in decent running condition. One very busy day I was running between two ministry locations, one in the suburbs and one in Center City Philadelphia. In rush-hour traffic my once-dependable minivan began to make a scary sound. It sounded like something was grinding against something it wasn't meant to grind against. Next, with the sound getting louder and my car beginning to slow, the thing began to jerk violently. When smoke appeared, I looked for a place to pull over and, just as I did, my minivan let out a final gasp and died. I knew then and there it was done. There would be no more restorative maintenance. As I sat in the car, I was beyond discouraged. We needed a car. I had no money. I couldn't even pay someone to tow my dead car to its final resting place. Cars honked as they drove around me, and I just sat wondering what I was going to do now.

Things fade and die; such is life in this fallen world. Things that we could once depend on, we can depend on no longer. In our personal histories stand mounds of defunct items, monuments in our memories of things that finally failed us. We all have our stories of cars, appliances, tools, and so on, that failed us, often when it seemed we needed them the most. We've learned not to expect things to last forever, and we're no longer surprised when they don't. Some people duct-tape and screw things back together in an attempt to fight the decay that is inevitable.

But this is true not just of things. People fade and die and, when we bury them, it feels like we bury so much of ourselves with them. Luella and I often talk about how we wish our parents were still with us. There are things we want to ask them, memories we would like to share, and present accomplishments they would find joy in. But death has taken them from us, and there can be no more conversations this side of forever.

Sometimes things other than death take treasured friends and loved ones from us. They move away and we say we'll stay in contact, but we don't. Dear friends become part of our history, never again to live with us in the present. I wish it were just time and space that separated us from people we held dear, but darker things get in the way. Jealousy darkens friendship, betrayal erodes trust, and rejection leaves us heartbroken and feeling alone. Sometimes we experience the joy of restorations and reconciliation, but other times the relationships seem irreparable. Some of us have been abused by those who should have been our protectors and providers. This makes it hard for us to trust, and it causes us to wonder when we will be hurt again. It's sad when physical things fail us, but a much deeper sadness results when those we entrusted ourselves to fail. The reality is that everyone will fail us in some way, and we too will fail them.

In this fallen world it is hard for us to believe that good things won't somehow, someway fail us in the end. Some of us live self-protectively, choosing to be alone rather than risking being hurt once again. Some of us allow the hurts of the past to control the way we deal with people and situations in the present. Some of us have come to the point where it is hard for us to believe that God won't fail us too.

One of the most important functions of corporate worship is to present to you again and again that our heavenly Father is unlike anyone you have known before. He is the definition of everything that is wise, loving, and good. It is impossible for him to fail you, because he is perfect in every way and all of the time. He never looks at his children with disgust and walks away. He never fails to keep every one of his promises. He never regrets that he has showered his love on you. He never gets frustrated with you and withdraws his grace. He never fails to meet every one of your needs. On your very worst day, he still showers you with his love. It is never risky to trust him. He doesn't offer you just his love, but with it he offers his guidance, protection, and a commitment to your personal transformation. Your Savior is a better friend than you could ever dream of having.

So we gather Sunday after Sunday to be reminded again that God is not like any friend we have ever known. In his faithful love, real life is found. In his faithful love, our hearts can finally rest with a peace that passes understanding. We gather to worship and remember that friend of friends who has found us and will hold us to his heart forever. "Greater love has no one than this, that someone lay down his life for his friends" (John 15:13).

———

Scripture: Habakkuk 3:17–19

Reflections: Take a moment to rest in the fact that God never fails to meet every one of your needs.

Family Discussion: Has someone or something failed you in the past, and does that affect your confidence in God?

Sunday 18

*Corporate worship is designed to remind you again and
again where true cleansing of heart and life is to be found.*

Like a bad stain on
white linen.
Like a black smudge on
pure vellum.
Like wine spilt on
a new dress.
Like paint drips on
window glass.
Like mud on
a new shoe.
This stain won't just
go away.
It won't fade into
nothing.
You won't wake up one
morning to discover

it has suddenly
disappeared.
The deepest,
darkest,
most penetrating,
stubborn stains
must be cleansed.
Denying that they're there
never works.
Doing your best to hide them
doesn't remove them.
Living with them
is foolishness.
Hoping no one will notice
is vain.
Worrying about them
changes nothing.
Whatever has been stained
must be cleansed
to be new again.
So it is with the human heart.
It is sad to admit,
but no one has a
pure,
perfectly clean,
unstained,
pristinely beautiful
heart.
No one.
Every heart of

every person
comes into this world
stained by sin.
Sin is immorality's
permanent ink,
sinking into the deepest regions
of the thoughts,
the desires,
the motives,
the purposes,
the worship
of the heart.
This tragic sin stain is
humanly unremovable.
No matter what you attempt,
no matter how many times you try,
sin is there to stay,
without something that has the power
to finally cleanse it.
But you can look at your stains with hope,
because
there is a cleansing stream.
It flows through the righteous life,
the substitutionary sacrifice,
the victorious resurrection of
Jesus.
He came so that sin-stained hearts
would have the hope
of being clean again,
new again,

spotless in his sight again,
one day completely pure again,
forever.
If we confess that we are
stained,
he is faithful,
he is righteous,
he will forgive our sins.
He will cleanse our hearts,
and thoroughly wash us
from all unrighteousness.
Step out from the shame of your
stains.
Refuse to put your hope in things
that do not cleanse.
Walk away from a life of denial.
Confess that you have no
cleansing power of your own.
Quit blaming your stains on
other people,
other things.
Humbly bring the garment of
your heart to him.
Put your stains in his hands.
He will wash you in his grace.
He delights in doing for you
what you could never do for yourself.
He delights in making you
clean.

May we never stop gathering to remember, to grow in understanding, and to deepen our celebration of the cleansing stream that is our Savior, Jesus.

—

Scripture: Psalm 32:5, Colossians 1:13–14, and 1 John 1:8–9

Reflections: Spend time in humble confession to our Savior, Jesus, who delights in making us clean.

Family Discussion: Discuss why we have no ability to cleanse ourselves.

Sunday 19

*Corporate worship is designed to move you
once again to live in the middle of the comfort
(grace) and call (discipleship) of the gospel.*

IT IS A BIT SHOCKING to think about, but Luella and I have been
married for fifty years. I can say without reservation that one of
the most wonderful and comforting things in my life is my knowledge that Luella loves me. And it's not just that I know it; I have
experienced her faithful and forgiving love for five decades of my
life. I asked her to marry me when I was seventeen. I understood
little about this thing called marriage and knew little about what
real love looked like. But Luella was willing to connect her heart
with mine and commit to a lifelong journey of love with me. It still
blows my mind that we have journeyed together this long and that
she still loves me to this day. Somehow I have not exhausted the
limits of her love. Somehow she still responds to me with patient
grace. Somehow she still enjoys our time together. Somehow she
is still ready to forgive me when I have failed her once again. Apart
from my relationship with God, nothing brings me greater pleasure

than her love. I will never tire of Luella saying to me, "I love you." I am so grateful that I am privileged to daily experience her love.

As a young man, it didn't take long to realize that it was not enough for me to bask in Luella's love. I learned early that romance isn't the cause of a good and heathy marriage. No, romance is the *result* of a good and healthy marriage. We entered our marriage because we loved one another, but that love needed to be nurtured and maintained. A good marriage is good because the people in that marriage have accepted the call to a marriage work ethic. You can't just coast your way through a love relationship. I love seeing older couples who clearly are best friends, clearly enjoy one another, and clearly have a strong union. I love seeing this because I know what it means. They have not just celebrated the comfort of marital love, but they have taken up the call of marital work and, because they have, they have a marriage that is healthy, vibrant, strong, and full of joy.

I have also learned that marriage is a picture of our union with our Savior. Like marriage, the gospel is also a comfort and a call. It's right to rest in, bask in, and celebrate the comfort of the gospel of Jesus Christ. Nothing is greater than being a child of God by grace. Consider:

All of your sins have been forgiven—past, present, and future.
God is with you and will never leave you.
He welcomes you to cast your cares on him.
He will never turn a deaf ear to your cries for help.
He draws you near with convicting grace.
He blesses you with his power.
His grace meets you in your weakness.
He gifts you with empowering and transforming grace.

He rules over all things for your sake.
He guards and protects you.
He meets all of your needs.
He loves you with a love that cannot be broken.
He has secured for you a place in his final kingdom.

It is amazing to get up in the morning and to know that these truths define you, your life, your potential, and your future. And it is mind-boggling to remember that all of these things are yours not because you deserved them, but because in eternity past God set his love on you. In all of life there is no greater comfort than to know that you have been loved by God. That love changes you and everything about you. So it is right for you to join the eternal celebration of the saints. In fact, because of who God is and for what he has done on our behalf, we should be the most celebratory community on earth. Every time we gather, we celebrate the one who has lavished such comforts on us, and we gather to celebrate that we really are the children of God. It simply doesn't get any better than this.

But between the "already" and the "not yet," it is spiritually dangerous to celebrate the comfort of the gospel without answering its call. No, your work does not get you greater acceptance with God. You have his complete and secure acceptance because of what Jesus has done for you in his life, death, and resurrection. But the Christian life is not designed to be a passive existence any more than passivity in marriage is a good thing. There is more grace to receive and more gospel work to be done. Grace is not finished with me, and God's worldwide mission of redemption is not yet complete.

The book of Ephesians divides itself into two clear sections. Chapters 1–3 present the most beautiful portrait of the comforts of the gospel. You could spend a lifetime unpacking the grace of Jesus on your behalf described in these chapters. But take note of how Paul kicks off the second section of Ephesians: "I therefore, a prisoner of the Lord, urge you to walk in a manner worthy of the calling to which you have been called" (Eph. 4:1). Paul wants the Ephesian believers to know that the gospel is not just a comfort— and praise God that it is—but it is also a call. What is that call? It is to live in light of the gospel in every dimension of your life. For Paul, the gospel sets the agenda for:

How I should live in the church.
What I should think and desire.
How I should live with and relate to others.
How I should talk.
What I should do with my money.
My sexuality.
How I should conduct myself in my marriage.
How I should parent my children.
How I should act in the workplace.
How I should arm myself for the inevitable spiritual warfare.

The call of the gospel reorients and reshapes our thoughts, desires, words, and actions in every area of our lives. So we come into the corporate gathering with our brothers and sisters bruised, wounded, and feeling guilty and defeated, and we need to hear again the amazing comforts of the gospel of Jesus Christ. We also come in with hearts that have wandered and lives that have been way too passive, and we need to hear again the call of the gospel. We gather to be comforted as we remember that God loves us and to remember that he has called us to a way of living that is infinitely better than anything we would have chosen for ourselves.

———

Scripture: Ephesians 2:8–10

Reflections: In what ways have you possibly grown passive in living out the gospel in everyday life?

Family Discussion: Choose one item from the list of comforts, and share why it is especially meaningful to you. Do the same for the list of ways to live in light of the gospel.

Sunday 20

Corporate worship is designed to help us remember the grace we easily forget when we succumb to the deadly combination of busyness and self-righteousness.

FROM A DISTANCE, Sam looked like he was doing well. He was married with three children, seemed active in his church, and enjoyed a successful career. Those who didn't know him well looked at him with respect. He seemed to have it all. But behind closed doors the picture was very different. In ways that he was blind to, his world was progressively coming unglued. His marriage was increasingly dysfunctional. He and Sally spent almost no time together. And when they were together, he was too distracted, too impatient, and too irritated to actually relate to his wife in a loving way. For several years she had tried to talk to him about the state of their marriage, but he was virtually unapproachable. He was good at turning the tables and reminding Sally that there was plenty of evidence that he wasn't the only sinner in the room. Their conversations almost always devolved into a litany of all of Sally's sin, weaknesses, and failures. Sally had quit trying to have those conversations and just tried to stay out of Sam's way to avoid being told, once again, what a bad person she was.

One reason their conversations were never productive was that Sam was a human biblical-doctrine think tank. He had a high level of biblical literacy, and he would tell Sally that there was nothing she could tell him from Scripture that he didn't already know. He had no understanding that if your theology makes you arrogant and unapproachable, it's bad theology. Sam had no clue that it is quite possible to use the Bible unbiblically. Something else caused Sam to be less than open in those hard conversations: he equated biblical literacy and theological expertise with personal spiritual maturity. But he was a living example of the fact that you can know the Bible and theology well and not be following God well in your everyday life.

Yet another component contributed to the worsening home mess. Sam was an absentee father. He had never been a parental presence in his kids' lives. He got up and went to work before they got out of bed and came home after they had gone to bed for the night. They didn't know him, and he didn't really know them. He was fully committed to the pursuit of business success. He had a dream of what that success would look like. This dream got him up in the morning and occupied him until very late at night. For a few years Sally would wait up for him, but he came in tired, with little patience for the report of her day or for her questions about his. So Sally quit staying up. The kids had become increasingly resentful of his absence and even more resentful that, when he was around, he tried to insert himself into things he hadn't been around for and didn't understand. All of them would have much rather had a dad who was present and involved than all the money and things he threw at them. But Sam was not just too busy for his family; he had little time for God. This man who once consumed his Bible barely picked it up anymore, and his need to miss Sunday worship was increasing. The things of God no longer filled his heart, shaped his conversations, or set the agenda for his life with his family. Sam lived at the intersection of busyness and self-righteousness and, if he continued, things would only worsen.

I don't think Sam is alone. These are spiritual dangers for all of us. Think with me for a moment. God has set significant time limits for each of us. You and I will never get thirty hours in a day, we will never get ten days in a week, we will never get fifty days in a month, and we will never get four hundred and fifty days in a year. Within the time limits God has set for us, we are called to a careful stewardship of three dimensions of our lives: spiritual (relationship with God and the surrender of your life to him); relational (relationship with family, brothers and sisters in Christ, and friends); and vocational (world of work). If one of these areas grows and grows, the increasing time investment in that area has to eat into other areas of your life, because you will never have time added to your day or an extra day added to your week. As the work commitments and the lure of success took up more of Sam's time, they ate into his time with his family and his Lord. More and more of work meant less and less of Sally and the kids and less and less devotional and worship time. Sam knew the Two Great Commandments well (Matt. 22:37–40), but the time demands of his career dreams daily caused him to break them both. Vertical and horizontal love were sacrificed at the altar of success, but Sam didn't see it.

The crisis of Sam's busyness was worsened by his self-righteousness. Because he was no longer looking in the mirror of God's word and seeing himself with accuracy, Sam had a distorted view of himself. This self-righteous man stood in the middle of a growing family disaster, but he couldn't see it. And when he did have a flash of insight, he would quickly blame someone or something else. Sam was simply too busy and too righteous to see and confess the need for change.

You see in Sam's story the genius of God's gift of sabbath. We all desperately need sabbath from our labors, but not just so we can physically rest and rejuvenate. We need sabbath so we can see clearly again, confess our need again, turn to grace again, and surrender again our self-glory to the greater glory of our Savior King. We all need regular moments when our bodies and minds are taken away, by grace, from our work and we sit with our brothers and sisters at the feet of our Savior, being confronted by how much we need his grace and being encouraged by its forgiving, transforming, and restoring power. We all need to step out of the busyness that occupies so much of our time and to gaze once again on the glorious glory of our Lord, remembering that all things are from him, through him, and to him (Rom. 11:36). We need to remember that God is at the center and we are not, and that this is a very good thing. So take time this week with your fellow believers to make sabbath. Rest, remember, confess, worship, and surrender. No matter how mature you may grow in the faith, you will never outgrow your need for the grace of sabbath.

———

Scripture: Matthew 22:36–40

Reflections: From the above passage, why do you think Jesus chose these specific commandments as the greatest?

Family Discussion: Which of the three dimensions of your life (spiritual, relational, or vocational) has to be monitored most carefully in order to keep a balance in your life?

Sunday 21

*Corporate worship is designed to produce in you
a greater sadness than you've felt before (sin),
resulting in deeper joy than you've known before
(grace), together producing more commitment to
God's will than you've had before (holiness).*

WHILE I WAS AWAY for a few days to do some recording, I received
an unexpected call. I could tell from the quiver in Luella's voice
that I was about to hear bad news. She told me that I needed to
get home as fast as I could because our daughter had been hit by
a car that had careened up onto the sidewalk and had crushed her
against a wall. By God's grace she was alive, although suffering
from multiple and potentially life-altering injuries. As I made the
six-hour trip home, my heart would sink every time my phone
rang. I don't know a time in my life when I have feared bad news
more. I'll never forget walking into that intensive care room and
seeing the broken body of my girl, lying there looking so tragically
fragile. Thankfully, my daughter recovered well and is now years
beyond the trauma of those days.

We instinctively dread bad news, and whatever dramatic life changes bad news will force upon us. I am persuaded that this is one of the reasons we must revisit the gospel of Jesus Christ. The gospel greets us with the worst news ever. The bad news the gospel gives us is particularly hard to accept because it is bad news about *us*. It's not the kind of bad news you know is going to introduce a hard season to walk through but that will someday end. No, this bad news is about something that is constitutionally, intrinsically wrong with us. The gospel forces us to face the fact that there is something deeply wrong with us that a change in situation, location, relationship, or behavior can't change. I can't educate myself out of it. Therapy won't deliver me from it. I have a disease that leads to death and, if left to myself, there is nothing I can do about it.

The gospel must confront me with my sin, or I will have no interest in its glorious message of grace. But I don't naturally think of myself as a sinner. The very sin which is my inescapable problem deceives me into thinking that I am okay. I may think someone else needs this bad news, but not me. This is why the Bible speaks about sin with such strong, all-inclusive language:

As it is written:

> "None is righteous, no, not one;
>> no one understands;
>> no one seeks for God.
> All have turned aside; together they have become worthless;
>> no one does good,
>> not even one."
> "Their throat is an open grave;
>> they use their tongues to deceive."

"The venom of asps is under their lips."
"Their mouth is full of curses and bitterness."
"Their feet are swift to shed blood;
   in their paths are ruin and misery,
   and the way of peace they have not known."
"There is no fear of God before their eyes."
(Rom. 3:10–18)

This very bad news of the gospel is communicated to us because of God's redeeming love. God works though his word, through his people, and through the gathering of his church to break through the impassable walls of our blindness to show ourselves as we actually are. If you were near someone who was carrying something deadly inside of him, wouldn't you agree that it would be unloving not to tell him? So God, in the majesty of his redeeming love, confronts us with what none of us wants to hear. He does this not because he despises us, but because he looks on us with a tender and compassionate heart. His bad news is rescuing news, delivered forcefully so that we will hear it, accept it, and reach out for the help that he alone can give.

The very bad news of the gospel is an introduction to the best news ever. God would not leave us in the sorry state of our sin. He was unwilling to condemn his world and walk away, because he abounds in mercy. So, he acted on our behalf by providing a way not only for our sin to be forgiven, but for us to be finally and completely delivered from sin. The gospel tells us that God sent his Son to live the perfectly righteous life that sin made impossible for us to live. It tells us that Jesus came to earth to be our sacrificial Lamb, taking the punishment for our sin on himself and, in so doing, satisfying God's anger. It further tells us that Jesus rose from the grave, conquering sin and death on our behalf. Because of the work of Jesus, we can be reconciled to God, adopted into his family, and guaranteed a place with him in eternity.

> For while we were still weak, at the right time Christ died for the ungodly. For one will scarcely die for a righteous person—though perhaps for a good person one would dare even to die—but God shows his love for us in that while we were still sinners, Christ died for us. Since, therefore, we have now been justified by his blood, much more shall we be saved by him from the wrath of God. For if while we were enemies we were reconciled to God by the death of his Son, much more, now that we are reconciled, shall we be saved by his life. More than that, we also rejoice in God through our Lord Jesus Christ, through whom we have now received reconciliation. (Rom. 5:6–11)

The bad news, good news, comfort, and call of the gospel is meant to produce in us a deep heart- and life-shaping commitment of gratitude to our Lord. It is meant to call us into a greater dependency on and surrender to him that results in a determination to live in a way that is holy in his sight—not because we fear his anger, but because we are the children of his love.

The church and its regular gatherings have been given to us because we cannot hear this gospel enough. We will continue to need its warning, encouragement, and motivation until we are on the other side and our struggle with sin is no more.

Scripture: Romans 3:23; 6:23, and Psalms 32:5; 32:1–2; 30:11–12

Reflections: Read the above verses in order and consider the progression from confrontation of sin to grace and holy living.

Family Discussion: Discuss how the gospel is not just hearing once and believing, but it is something we cannot hear enough.

Sunday 22

*Corporate worship is designed to remind you that
you have been welcomed to place your cares on
the capable shoulders of your Savior King.*

AS EMMA WALKED into my office, she looked like she was carrying
the weight of the world on her shoulders. I didn't even have a chance
to greet her before she blurted out, "I just don't know what I'm
going to do." She was watching her marriage fall apart, but despite
all her efforts to restore it and reconcile with her husband, it was
now worse than it had ever been. She told me she couldn't live like
this and that for the last few days all she wanted to do was to die.

———

The bullying Jamie endured at school seemed more intense than
ever. He didn't want to talk too much about it with his parents
because he didn't want to worry them. He was afraid to go to the
school counselor because he thought that if the bullies found out,
they would go after him even more. One morning his alarm rang,

but he didn't get out of bed. He couldn't face another day at school. He pulled the covers over his head in an attempt to deny the sad realities of his teenage life.

———

Bill didn't have much money, he worked a job he didn't really like, and he didn't have much of a circle of friends. But what burdened him the most was the huge weight of regret he carried with him every day. It was like a backpack of rocks waiting at the foot of his bed that he put on every day when he got up. He had made so many bad choices as a teenager, and now he was paying the price. Everything he did was marred by guilt and shame. He just couldn't seem to chuck the burden. He ended every day completely exhausted by the burden of the regret, guilt, and shame he constantly carried.

———

Charlotte had been the single woman at too many weddings. She hated when she got another invitation to another friend's wedding. It made her envious, it made her mad, and it made her wonder what in the world was wrong with her. She was way beyond high school and college, where she had dated a bit. Now there were few available men in her life, and those who were acted as if they didn't know she existed. She knew she shouldn't be bitter, but she was. She knew there were many blessings in her life, but she was still discontent. She was tired of the burden of being alone.

———

Steve had a dark and scary secret that he would never tell. He knew that to confess this secret would mean the end of all the good things in his life. But carrying it alone was a huge and unbearable burden. He was in his second year of college, and he was more attracted to the other men in his dorm than he was to the many available women on campus. Since midway through high school he had denied these feelings. His time in youth groups was terrifying because he thought somehow he would give his secret away. It seemed impossible to tell his parents or his friends. He had considered talking to his pastor, but was too afraid of what he would say or do. The guys around him didn't understand why he didn't date, telling him that there were lots of women on campus who would love to spend time with him. He was running out of excuses and was tired of how exhausting it was to carry the burden of this secret alone.

———

Each of these people is suffering not just from carrying burdens of life in a broken, groaning world, but because they are shouldering these heavy burdens alone. It is true that life between the "already" and the "not yet" is marked by burdensome moments. Perhaps that burden is a particular temptation that seems to stalk and haunt you. Maybe it's the burden of human rejection or the loss of a dear loved one. It could be that the burden is the death of a dream. Perhaps it's the doors that are closed to you because of your faith. Maybe your burden is physical weakness or financial want. It could be that you're dealing with the crushing burden of a family that has been shattered by sin and anger. Maybe it's the burden of a boss who makes every day of your work life harder than it otherwise would be. Maybe it's a church that is gone because of leaders who lost their way. Maybe your burden is anxiety, fear, or depression. We all carry burdens that we, thankfully, will no longer carry once grace has finally and forever led us to the other side.

Our Creator did not design us for independent living. There is no greater, more destructive lie than the one told by the serpent in the garden, that is, that Adam and Eve could live well apart from dependence upon the one who made them. Human independence is a delusion that will take you nowhere good. So we need to have our instinct for independence confronted again and again. And we need to hear this invitation again and again: ". . . casting all your anxieties on him, because he cares for you" (1 Pet. 5:7). God has designed for us to gather with one another again and again precisely because we are weak and needy people who were not designed for independent living. As we gather, we remember again that there is one who cares for us and who is both willing and capable of meeting us in our moment of burden and doing in us and for us what no one else would be able to do. We gather to remember that our Lord understands what we are going through, because for thirty-three years he walked in our shoes, experiencing all the burdens we now experience. We gather to remember that he is tender. Isaiah tells us that "a bruised reed he will not break, and a faintly burning wick he will not quench" (42:3). He rules all the situations and locations where we carry those anxieties, burdens, and cares. He is present with us always, promising to never leave or forsake us. His grace is inexhaustible, his love is boundless, and his mercies are new every morning. We gather to remember that God's grace doesn't move us from dependence to independence, but from independence to a humble, joyful dependence on our Savior. So as we come together week after week, tired and needy, reaching again for his help, he receives us with tender grace and he willingly shoulders burdens we are unable to bear alone.

———

Scripture: Psalm 55:22 and Lamentations 3:19–24

Reflections: Is there a heavy burden that you have been shouldering alone that you need to hand over to the Lord?

Family Discussion: Why do you think Satan wants us to believe the lie that human independence is a good thing? Discuss the comforting words in the above passages.

Sunday 23

*Corporate worship is designed to make us
celebrate the soaking rain of God's grace
that pours down on us every day.*

IT WAS A COLD SPRING DAY in New York City. I was there with
two of my friends for the day to see the Big Apple sights, have a great
meal, and then hop on the train back to Philadelphia. The day before
had been a beautiful East Coast spring day: birds, spring flowers, and
lots of sunshine. When we walked up the stairs out of Penn Station,
we noticed some dark clouds, but we hoped for the best. But in the
middle of a short walk through Central Park, it began to rain. The rain
was light at first, but soon it was pouring, with little shelter in sight.
I was soaked, cold, and irritated. When we finally sat down for dinner,
we were a dripping sight to behold. We've looked back and laughed
about that day, but it was anything but funny at the time.

Most of us don't really like rain. We do our best to avoid it, even
to the extent of canceling activities. And when we can't avoid it, we
go out armed with umbrellas and dressed in rain gear. However, in
biblical times rain was considered a blessing:

Be glad, people of Zion,
    rejoice in the LORD your God,
for he has given you the autumn rains
    because he is faithful.
He sends you abundant showers,
    both autumn and spring rains, as before. (Joel 2:23 NIV)

Because of this, rain became a word picture for God's blessing:

I will pour water on the thirsty land,
    and streams on the dry ground;
I will pour my Spirit on your offspring,
    and my blessing on your descendants. (Isa. 44:3)

There is a rain that is vastly more important than the physical rain that waters dry land. It is spiritual rain, that is, the never-ceasing rain of the resources of God's grace that alone is able to water and nourish parched and weakened souls.

With grace we never have a dry season. The grace of God in Christ Jesus is an inexhaustible flow of spiritual nutrients. God never stops pouring out his Spirit on his children. He never stops meeting us with sustaining grace. New mercies from his hand rain on us every morning. Showers of blessings never stop falling. We are kept alive spiritually by the constant rain of his grace. It is the best of all blessings; it is good to be chosen to be soaked in the rain of redeeming grace.

Romans 8:18–39 gives us one of Scripture's most beautiful and encouraging descriptions of God's grace. We gather week after week to remember passages like this and to celebrate that we have been chosen to be soaked by God's grace, saturated with his love, and drenched in his mercy. Let's consider how this passage helps us understand the essentiality of the grace that rains down on the children of God.

Verses 18–25 give us the context in which that grace operates. Paul's description here would be scary and disheartening if it were not for the hope of the verses that follow. Between the "already" of our conversion and the "not yet" of our homegoing, Paul wants us to know that we are living in a terribly broken world that does not function as God originally intended. We are living in a world that is groaning, waiting for redemption. We live in a place that has been subjected to futility and is in constant bondage to decay, where suffering is a universal experience, and so we too groan, crying out for redemption.

The Old Testament would call our present address a dry and parched land, one that desperately needs the rain of God's grace, the rain of life-giving nutrients that is ours in Christ. The attributes of that rain of grace are beyond encouraging, especially in the face of the hardships of life in a groaning world.

What is the nature of the grace that God pours down on his children?

God blesses us with intervening grace (Rom. 8:26–27). Sometimes life is so distressing, so confusing, so surprising, and so multifaceted that, in our confusion, we don't know how to pray or what to pray for. But we are not left in our distress to make it on our own, because God meets us by his Spirit. The Spirit intercedes for us, carrying our needs to the Father. Because of the rain of intervening grace, we don't have to fear our weakness, distress, or confusion. God doesn't look on us with disgust but provides, in his Spirit, just the help we need. Because our Lord pours abundant grace down on his children, we should not be afraid of coming to

God in weakness; what we should be afraid of are our delusions of independent spiritual strength.

God blesses us with unstoppable grace (Rom. 8:28–30). No matter how hard life seems, no matter how weak we may be, and no matter how parched our souls may become, nothing can stop the eternal march of God's grace. His mission of redemption will not stop until every microbe of sin is removed from every cell of every heart of every one of his children. None of his children will be lost along the way; all will finally be formed into his image. This means that right now God is pouring down his rescuing, forgiving, transforming, empowering, and delivering grace on each one of us. We may get weary and tired, and our commitment may weaken, but God's redeeming grace never tires and the commitment of our Savior to finally complete his work will never, ever wane.

God blesses us with providing grace (Rom. 8:31–32). Paul's words about God's provision here are enormously encouraging. He poses this rhetorical question: If God would go to the radical extent of sacrificing his Son for our redemption, then won't he also graciously give us all things? The answer is, "Of course." What sense would it make for God to march all of history toward the life, death, and resurrection of his Son and then abandon his redeemed children? The past grace of the cross is our guarantee of the rain of present and future grace. This grace will supply everything we need right here, right now. God never stops raining down provision on his children.

God blesses us with inseparable grace (Rom. 8:33–39). This is where Paul's description of the elements and operation of God's grace reaches its crescendo. Paul wants us to know that nothing—that's right, nothing—in heaven or on earth has the power to separate us from the love of God in Christ Jesus our Lord. We did not earn that love and we are not now earning it. This love, which is eternally and inseparably ours, was placed on us before the foundations of the earth were set in place and will be ours into the endless eons of eternity.

Why is this Paul's crescendo? Because he knows that all human beings wonder if they will be loved and further wonder if they will still be loved once they are known. The answer for the child of God is, "Yes and yes!" We are loved with an everlasting love that cannot and will not be broken.

So the next time you step out into the rain, remember the incessant rain of God's intervening, unstoppable, providing, and inseparable grace. Look up into the sky and be glad that there is another rain, a gift of God that you could never achieve, earn, or deserve—the rain of his redeeming grace. And remember that God has designed the gatherings of his church to be a place where his dry and parched children can step into his rain and repeatedly be soaked in his grace.

Scripture: Ezekiel 34:26

Reflections: Which aspect of the nature of God's grace is most comforting to you at this point in your life?

Family Discussion: Talk about why the Bible uses *showers* to describe grace and blessings.

Sunday 24

*Corporate worship is designed to remind us that
weakness does not hinder God's plan; it is the plan, so
that God's all-surpassing power will shine through.*

ONE OF SCRIPTURE'S most encouraging and motivating passages
is found in 2 Corinthians 4.

But we have this treasure in jars of clay, to show that the surpassing power belongs to God and not to us. We are afflicted in
every way, but not crushed; perplexed, but not driven to despair;
persecuted, but not forsaken; struck down, but not destroyed;
always carrying in the body the death of Jesus, so that the life of
Jesus may also be manifested in our bodies. For we who live are
always being given over to death for Jesus' sake, so that the life
of Jesus also may be manifested in our mortal flesh. So death is
at work in us, but life in you.

So we do not lose heart. Though our outer self is wasting
away, our inner self is being renewed day by day. For this light
momentary affliction is preparing for us an eternal weight of

glory beyond all comparison, as we look not to the things that are seen but to the things that are unseen. For the things that are seen are transient, but the things that are unseen are eternal. (2 Cor. 4:7–12, 16–18)

We gather for worship so that these counterintuitive gospel realities will increasingly become the way we view ourselves and the hardships we face. We need to be reminded again and again that spiritual maturity is not about the assurance of personal strength; it is about being joyfully willing to admit weakness, because of the constant renewing work of God's grace in our lives. We should not fear the weakness that drives us into our Lord's hands. What we should fear are the delusions of strength that tempt us to live independently.

Meditate on the words that follow.

I am weary,
but not defeated.
I am tired,
but not without strength.
I am beaten down,
but not crushed.
I am misunderstood,
but not disappointed.
I am often confused,
but not given to doubt.
I often am at the end of my rope,
but I never give up.
I don't know how to pray,
but you hear my cries.

I am sometimes friendless,
but I am never alone.
I am often without power,
but I do not lack strength.
I have little control,
but my life is not out of control.
My heart is hungry,
but I am constantly filled.
I carry heavy burdens,
but I am not overwhelmed.
When I am rejected,
you are near.
When I am fearful,
you give me peace.
When I am distressed,
you are my comfort.
When I am confused,
you are my wisdom.
When I fail,
you are my forgiveness.
When I face temptation,
you are my protector.
When I am hopeless,
you are my encouragement.
When I am burdened,
you are my helper.
I have come to understand that
I should not fear weakness.
My weakness is a workroom
for your grace.

Your plan is for me to be
a broken vessel
so your power
gets attention,
so you are celebrated,
so you are worshiped,
so you get praise
and not me.
So I will never give up.
I will not lose heart.
When I am wasting away,
I will remember
this glorious truth:
I am being renewed day by day.

May we gather, gather, and gather again as the humble company
of the weak, welcomed into the presence of the one who is strength,
and celebrate the renewal that only he can give.

Scripture: 2 Corinthians 12:9–10

Reflections: From the above verses, why is Paul able to boast in his
weaknesses rather than complain or allow them to hinder his work?

Family Discussion: From the 2 Corinthians 4 passage, what is
meant by *this treasure* and *jars of clay*? Why is this counterintuitive?

Sunday 25

Corporate worship is meant to make you weep with
sadness (over sin) and celebrate with joy (over grace).

"BLESSED ARE THOSE WHO MOURN, for they shall be comforted"
(Matt. 5:4). We don't tend to like to be sad. We hate bad news.
We work to avoid problems. We apologize when we cry in
public. Being depressed scares us. In our avoidance of sadness,
we often numb ourselves to death with endless social media
fluff and vacuous Netflix entertainment. Perhaps what we're
running from is not just sadness; perhaps we're running from
ourselves. Perhaps we're running from what we would be forced
to acknowledge if we took the time to stop, look, and listen.
Running from your true self is never a good life plan. But that
is what the powerful media platforms allow and perhaps even
encourage us to do. They spirit us away from the pain of honest life consideration and humble introspection. Perhaps our
media busyness is yet another distraction that stands in the way
of blessing, the kind of blessing that comes only when we stop,
consider, reflect, and mourn.

When is the last time you mourned? I don't mean mourning that your team lost or that your steak wasn't that great. I'm not talking about being sad that you children aren't quick to obey or that your marriage hasn't lived up to your dreams. I don't mean the type of mourning that happens when the house deal falls through, the investment tanks, or your job ends. I think we all do a lot of mourning, but it tends to be little-kingdom mourning. What is little-kingdom mourning? Remember Jesus's words about mourning from his Sermon on the Mount (Matt. 5:4). These are followed by Christ's instruction on how we should pray: "Your kingdom come, your will be done, on earth as it is in heaven" (Matt. 6:10). Jesus instructs us to pray in willing submission to a kingdom that is vastly greater than our little kingdoms of one.

The kingdom of self is concerned about our wants, our needs, and our feelings. Its primary focus is our comfort, pleasure, and satisfaction. It is consumed by our dreams for our lives, that is, the things that we think would be easy and enjoyable. There is nothing wrong with wanting a good marriage or obedient children. There would be something wrong with you if you didn't want these things. But it's wrong and spiritually dangerous to have your heart controlled by the desire for these things in a way that causes you to be perennially discontent. Here's the point. What you regularly and deeply mourn will always reveal the true values of your heart. What causes the most sadness will expose whatever kingdom has captured the allegiance of your heart. Mourning is a window into what we truly worship: the Creator or the created thing.

So I need to rephrase my previous question. It's not enough to ask when you last mourned. I need to ask, "What was it that you mourned the last time you mourned?" If Jesus is saying that mourning is a pathway to blessing, then it is vital to clarify what kind of mourning he's talking about. He is not talking about situational-disappointment mourning, where I am sad because something in a situation, location, or relationship didn't go as I hoped. This is the kind of mourning most of us are familiar with. We get upset when we don't get what we want. I call it little-kingdom mourning because it is all about human plans, purposes, and glory. This kind of mourning isn't a pathway to blessing. True happiness, blessing, and joy are never found when you make yourself the center of things. Putting your wants, needs, and feelings in the center is, in a fallen world, always a recipe for disappointment and discontent.

When Jesus says that mourners are blessed, he is talking about a kind of mourning that has God's purpose and glory in view. Romans 3:23 tells us the kind of mourning that Jesus is talking about: "For all have sinned and fall short of the glory of God." The admission of sin is at the heart of this kind of mourning. But there is more. I mourn because my sin is against God. It is a rebellion against his glory. It replaces his glory with my glory as the motivation for my living. Sin is a sad and shocking rejection of my identity as a creature of God as well as the purpose for my existence. I was designed to live in such a way that every thought, desire, choice, word, and action would be done with God's glory in view. It is devastatingly sad when any human being fails to live in this way. This failure not only denigrates the throne of God, but it leaves creation horribly damaged and causes untold human suffering. Sin is the saddest, most horrible thing that has ever happened. The cross tells us this. What could be more horrible than something that would necessitate the crucifixion of the Son of God?

Because of the hardness and blindness of the human heart, if you mourn your sin, if you see it as the saddest thing in your life, then you know that you have been visited by God's grace. But it is also true that only when you mourn your sin will you then seek and celebrate God's grace. The depth of your appreciation and gratitude for God's grace will be determined by the depth and consistency of your sadness over your sin. It really is true that whenever we minimize the horror of sin, we devalue the glory of God's amazing grace in Christ Jesus.

So we gather again and again not just to be encouraged but also to be confronted. We gather to be given eyes to see the shocking self-glory, darkness, deceitfulness, rebelliousness, and destructiveness of sin and to remember that sin still lives inside of us. We gather to remember that our only hope in the face of this evil is the powerful and ever-present grace of Jesus. It is when we acknowledge our sin that we experience the deepest and fullest of comforts. Yes, we gather again and again because we can never let ourselves forget that the greatest, most comforting oasis for a sinner's heart is the forgiving and transforming grace of Jesus.

———

Scripture: James 4:7–10

Reflections: What causes you to regularly and deeply mourn? What true values of your heart are revealed?

Family Discussion: What would life in our home look like if every thought, desire, choice, word, and action were done with God's glory in view? Does it cause you to mourn when you fail to live in this way?

Sunday 26

Corporate worship is designed to give you
eyes to see God and a heart that loves him
so that you will live in his service.

WHEN I WAS IN SEMINARY, Luella and I worked at a school for blind children. We were house parents of high school boys. Our school was designed to give these children the skills they needed to be successful as blind people in a sighted world. We were firsthand observers of what it meant to be blind from morning to evening, inside or outside, alone or with a group, in athletics or academics, and at work or leisure. We mourned that our boys would never see the blossoms of spring, dark rain clouds, the darting flight of a hummingbird, the beauty of an ocean sunset, a great painting, or the faces of family and friends. One boy explained to us that being blind is not like closing your eyes. When you close your eyes, you still see things, if only darkness. He said that the best way for a sighted person to experience blindness is to try to look out of the back of your head. Try it, and you will experience in a small way what it means to see nothing.

Physical blindness is a very sad thing. It alters everything you attempt to do in life. But there is a form of blindness that is profoundly sadder than physical blindness; it is God-blindness. It is a very sad thing that human beings would ever look at the world, others, or their own lives and not see the one who is the Creator and who sits at the center of it all. We were created to acknowledge God, worship him, and surrender our thoughts and desires to his will. But we cannot live as we were designed if we are functionally blind to his existence. God-blindness robs us of the very core of our identity and purpose as human beings made in the image of God.

The God-blindness that is most dangerous is not formal philosophical atheism. Here people argue against the evidences for the existence of God, saying that they put their trust in the "facts" of science instead of faith. Yes, philosophical atheism is a spiritually destructive thing, but there is a form of God-blindness that is so subtle and pervasive that it can capture even Bible-believing Christians. Functional atheism is way more dangerous than philosophical atheism, because it is possible to think that you're a God follower and yet, where the rubber meets the road in daily life, you live in areas of your life as if God does not exist. You might formally confess that you believe in God, but that belief fails to shape the way you use your money, or the way you approach your marriage or parenting, the kind of relationships you have with your neighbors, the way you define the "good life," your approach to job and career, the degree of involvement you have with your local church, or the way you truly think about what is important in life. Acknowledging the existence of God is never just a mental or theological thing. True biblical belief is never held separate from your daily life. What you truly believe is always revealed by how you live your life, that is, by the choices you make, the actions you take, and the values that shape how you spend your money and time.

Sadly, for many of us there is a gap between our confessional theology and our functional theology. So we get up in the morning and see the rising sun, but we fail to see in it the glory of God. We pray quick morning prayers, but don't really give our hearts to the worship of God or surrender our lives to him. We parent our children without really seeing ourselves as ambassadors of the one to whom our children belong or committing ourselves, in all of our actions and reactions as parents, to represent our Lord well. We see our money as belonging to us to provide for our needs and pleasures, while we give little back to God. In our work we see ourselves more as working for a paycheck than we think of the calling to work as unto the Lord. We approach church life more as consumers than as committed members of a ministering community. We sing songs about God's sacrificial generosity, but we fail to live sacrificially generous and hospitable lives.

We are bombarded by technology. We carry it in our pockets or purses and fill our homes with it. No wonder it's so easy to fall into God-blindness. Throughout most of the technological media landscape, God doesn't exist. The kind of life that social media and streaming sites push on us is one where human happiness is at the center of all things, where human beings define their own morality and where the existence, presence, purpose, rule, and glory of God is nonexistent. It is foolish to think that this 24/7 onslaught of comedic, dramatic, and informational content has no influence on us. We absorb the worldview of people who are God-blind way more than we absorb the content of those who have bowed their knees to the existence and majesty of God and who help us explore the life-commanding and life-shaping content of his word. Perhaps many of us are more blind than we think we are. Perhaps we have become all too comfortable living in a way that is not outrageously rebellious, yet does not constantly recognize God's existence and does not constantly grapple with what it means to live according to his will and for his glory in every dimension of life.

So we all need instruments of seeing in our lives that will help us recognize God at every turn and understand the functional difference between living for ourselves and living for him. The church has been designed to be one of God's primary instruments of God-sightedness. The church meets us in our vertical vision difficulty and hands us gospel glasses to put on. When we look through these glasses, we see God in all his glorious glory; we see Jesus the sacrificial Lamb; we see the Spirit, who lives within us, empowering us to do God's will; we see our desperate need for God's forgiving and empowering grace; we see our call to join God in his redemptive mission; and we see our calling to surrender everything in our hearts and lives to his will. We should all be thankful for the regular gathering of God's people for worship and instruction, because in some way we all still need our vision corrected and recorrected. We gather because we don't want to be blind in any way to the most important thing the eyes of the human heart could ever see: our great and glorious Lord.

Scripture: Psalm 119:18 and Revelation 3:17–18

Reflections: Consider the phrase "True biblical belief is never held separate from your daily life." In what area of your life do you most need your vision corrected?

Family Discussion: What kind of worldview are you absorbing through your use of technology? How can you expose yourself more to the life-shaping content of God's word?

Sunday 27

*Corporate worship is designed to give you a vertical
rest that is more powerful than the horizontal
difficulties you face in this fallen world.*

ONE OF THE RESULTS of my physical sickness was that I lost my
ability to sleep. I had always been a sound sleeper. I would hit
the bed, close my eyes, and fall into a deep and beautiful sleep.
But suddenly I couldn't sleep. It didn't help to get up, read a
book, look at my phone, or have a middle-of-the-night snack. So
I would lie still in bed with my eyes closed, but be wide awake,
often for the entire night. People asked me if I had anxious
thoughts, but I didn't. Often I would lie there and pray or think
about the book I was working on at the time. I tried every sleep
aid I could find, and I read everything about sleep I could get
my hands on, but nothing worked. If I got two nights a week
of restful sleep, I was grateful. It was so bad and so consistent
that I used to tell Luella that I was going to go upstairs and go
to "wake." This was one of the most difficult and discouraging
times of my life.

It is incredibly discouraging to wake up with important things to do, things that require mental and physical energy, but to wake up exhausted. It is hard to face a day when all you want to do is go to sleep. It is disheartening to be tired but to dread going to bed because you know you won't sleep. The ability of the body to rest is one of our loving Lord's good gifts to us. The fact that we have been hardwired to sleep is a priceless mercy. The fact that God has designed our bodies to go through a daily pattern of physical shutdown and regeneration is a demonstration of both his incalculable wisdom and his boundless love.

We are limited beings. We don't have endless physical, mental, emotional, or spiritual strength. We have not been designed to be "on" all the time. We regularly grow physically tired and mentally weary. We need rest from the emotional and spiritual burdens that we bear in this fallen world. Children, who don't know the value of rest and who seem to have limitless energy, often fight going to sleep. They protest when told to go to bed, they try every bargain at their disposal, they use every creative instinct they have to delay the process and, when finally in bed, they fight sleep. But there will come a time when they will love sleep, and no one will have to war with them to get to bed. There will come a time when their parents will battle for them to wake up and get out of bed.

I am sleeping much better now, and I am more grateful for the gift of nightly rest. I thank God every night for the gift of this thing called a bed and for the ability of my body to go to sleep. My bed and my sleep are constant reminders that God is good and that he loves me. But there is a rest I have been given that is way more important and life-giving than physical rest; it is the rest that is mine as a child of God. This rest addresses my deepest need.

My deepest problems are not physical, so my deepest need is for a rest that is deeper than physical rest. I was born in sin, and I carry its scars and burdens with me. I was born with an inability to live up to the standard of God's law. I was born into a world where temptation is all around me and the enemy prowls around looking to attack. I was born to be in relationship with God, but sin separated me from him and I had no power whatsoever to bridge that gap. I was created to live forever, but because of the horrible entrance of sin into the world, death is the sword of Damocles that hangs over me. I was created to have everything I think, desire, say, and do come from a pure heart, but my heart is not pure and my motives are often mixed. I was designed to love my neighbor, but often I am so busy loving myself that I have little time to even think about my neighbor. Apart from God's help, if left to myself I could not be what I was created to be or do what I was called to do. Sin separated me from God, for whom I was made, and made it impossible for me to live up to his will.

The double burden of sin and the law make life wearisome and discouraging. No wonder so many people are depressed, anxious, and angry. They may not understand why life is so hard or why they feel so alienated and alone, but God does and for that he sent his Son. Jesus came to give us a Sabbath of rest. He came to give us rest from the impossibility of defeating sin on our own and from our inability to live up to God's glorious commands. In his life, Jesus came to stand in our place and do what we could never do: perfectly keep God's law, all of the time and in every way. In his substitutionary death on the cross, Jesus satisfied God's anger with sin and, in his victorious resurrection, he defeated death. We don't have to perfectly obey God's law to have a relationship with him, because Jesus did it on our behalf. We do not have to fear God's anger, because Jesus took every bit of our penalty. And we do not have to live with the burdensome fear of death, because in Christ we have been granted eternal life. So, like the Sabbath created in the garden, we have been given, in Jesus, a sabbath of rest from our labors. Jesus has labored so efficiently and completely on our behalf that he was able to say, "It is finished" (John 19:30). We can rest because Jesus did for us all that needs to be done. "For if Joshua had given them rest, God would not have spoken of another day later on. So then, there remains a Sabbath rest for the people of God, for whoever has entered God's rest has also rested from his works as God did from his" (Heb. 4:8–10).

Every gathering of the people of God for worship and instruction is a celebration of that sabbath of rest. We gather again and again so we will never forget that we have been given the best rest ever: vertical, spiritual rest. It is ours not because we have worked hard, but because of the redeeming grace that is ours in Christ Jesus.

———

Scripture: Galatians 3:13–14 and Titus 3:4–6

Reflections: In what ways are you tempted to measure the quality of your relationship with God by your ability to perfectly obey his commands?

Family Discussion: What did Jesus accomplish in his life, death, and resurrection that enables us to rest?

Sunday 28

Corporate worship is designed to remind you that
you're not alone in this broken world. Immanuel,
the Lamb, the Prince of Peace is with you.

A MAN SAT IN MY OFFICE looking like he had been physically beaten up. I had never seen someone's body language so clearly communicate *defeated*. He looked at the floor more than he looked at me, and he mumbled responses to my questions. He told me he was tired of being alone. He hated going to work, because his accounting job was solitary. He would arrive, go to his cubicle, and begin a day that held little human interaction. He usually ate lunch at his desk because of the pressure of his workload. He dreaded the ride home in his car, because he knew he would arrive to an empty apartment and spend another long evening alone. His summary of his life went like this: "If I died today, no one would know and no one would care." As I listened to him, I knew he needed something deeper and more satisfying than human friends.

One of the saddest words in human language is *alone*. None of us like to be to left totally alone. We are sad when we have no one to laugh with, no one to cry with, and no one to turn to when we don't know what to do. All of us hunger for love. All of us want to be accepted, to know that we belong. All of us hate rejection. So many of the things that we're called to do are done better or are more enjoyable when we do them with others. We all need people in our lives who instruct us, guide us, mentor us, counsel us, and protect us. We haven't learned all that we know on our own, and we won't continue to learn and grow on our own. Many of the things we take credit for have actually depended on the contributions of others. For all of our love for the stirring stories of self-made people, human independence is a delusion. We don't want to have to make it on our own, and we dread ever having to close the door behind us with the knowledge that we have no one, that we are truly alone.

This is why few words are more beautifully heartening than God's words to his children: "I will never leave you nor forsake you" (Heb. 13:5). For the child of God there is no such thing as being truly alone. God walked with Adam and Eve in the garden; his glory filled the temple in Jerusalem; Jesus came as Immanuel, God with us; and the Spirit now lives inside of every believer. This is the radical, glorious, inescapable core of the hope of every Christian. It's not enough to say that God invites us into his presence by grace, though that is truly a glorious thing. Think of the Old Testament saints, singing the Songs of Ascent as they journeyed to the temple where God's presence dwelled. It was a beautiful grace that they were welcomed to be even near his presence. But there was a veil of separation between the children of God and the visible cloud of his glory. It was a moment of incredible grace when, at the moment of Christ's death on the cross, that veil was torn in two. Now, because of Jesus's sacrifice, the children of God were invited not just to the temple but into the actual presence of the Lord Almighty. We now dwell in his presence, invited to come to him by faith.

But there is more. The gospel is not just about God's welcoming us to come to him; it is also about the radical act of God's coming to us. The Word (Jesus) became flesh and dwelled among us (John 1:14). Think of it. God Almighty, the Creator, took on the form and shape of a human being and lived as a creature with the creatures he made. This historical reality is almost too mind-bending to grasp. To rescue us, he had to live with us, be like us, and be for us. The one who made us had to become our substitute, to live as we were unable to live, die in our place, and conquer death on our behalf.

Imagine the disciples' consternation when they began to grasp that Immanuel was leaving earth to ascend to the right hand of the Father. It was unthinkable that they would lose him again. But he would not leave them alone. He had come to dwell with them forever. So he left them with the promise of his Spirit, who would dwell within them forever. God with us is the hope of hopes. He has not only eternally forgiven us; he not only rules all things for our sake; he not only bestows on us his fatherly love and care; but he is *with* us. I know that I forget, I lose sight of, and I fail to recognize the grace of his constant presence. Sometimes I live as if it's me against the world. Sometimes, because I have forgotten him, I take credit for what I could have never achieved or produced on my own. I need the constant reminder of the amazing grace of Christ's presence, so he has ordained that his children would gather again and again around his throne to sing about, celebrate, and learn of the glory of his eternal presence with his people.

There is one more way that the gospel of Jesus Christ welcomes us out of our aloneness. God not only welcomes us to himself and he not only comes to dwell with us, but he gathers us together. The gospel is not an individual thing; it is a community thing. We are welcomed to a people—a communion, a fellowship—to be members of a body, stones in a temple, a family, brothers and sisters, together as the children of God. By grace, God creates for us the deepest and most precious of human connections—the church, that is, the interconnected body of Christ. Though we are different from one another, we have one profound thing in common. We have one Father, we are one family, and there is one Spirit who lives in each and every one of us. Grace has united us not just to God but to one another in a deep and eternal union. Every time we enter a house of worship and are greeted by our brothers and sisters, we are reminded that we are not alone. God has given us not only himself, but he has given us one another. It's hard to feel alone when you're surrounded by your loving family. That is reason enough for us to gather again and again. The more you feel connected to God and his family, the less you are susceptible to listening to the enemy ask, "Where is your God now?"

———

Scripture: Psalms 73:23; 139:17–18, and Isaiah 41:10

Reflections: During what times do you tend to forget the grace of God's constant presence? How can gathering with God's family remind us that we are not alone?

Family Discussion: Which of the names for Christ is a comfort to you when you feel alone?

Sunday 29

Corporate worship rescues us again and again
by reminding us that there's only one glory
worth giving our lives to: the glory of God.

DANIEL 4 RECORDS one of the most shocking moments in biblical history. It's important to note that this account was preserved for us by a loving God for the purpose of warning us and rescuing us. Nebuchadnezzar was the king of the most powerful nation on earth. He was so inflamed with his own glory that he essentially set himself up as an object of worship. He was a self-obsessed, murderous dictator. Yet God, in the richness of his mercy, chose to warn Nebuchadnezzar by means of a confusing and troubling dream and sent Daniel to interpret the dream. The dream was a warning to the king to turn from his self-glory obsessed iniquity. Now, we must note that if God's only intention was to judge this man, then God would never have warned him first. Every warning in Scripture is a sign of God's grace. Every warning helps us to see our sin more clearly and gives us an opportunity to confess and repent. God was, in fact, showing love to a man whom we would probably think clearly did not deserve God's love.

What happens next is equally amazing. We are told that God gave Nebuchadnezzar a year to decide whether he would heed God's warning, forsake his self-glory, and turn from his sin. Let this sink in. Meditate for a moment on the Lord's patience. If you are a parent, can you imagine commanding one of your children to do something and then allowing him to wait twelve months to do it? It usually takes us only a few minutes of delayed obedience for us to get angry. But our Lord is slow to anger and abounding in love and mercy. He lets his judgment wait so his grace has time to do its heart-altering work. He gives conviction time to break down our prideful, self-defending arguments for our righteousness. Every one of us experiences the grace of his patience every day of our lives.

Yet, after the double grace of God's warning and his patience, where do we find Nebuchadnezzar? We find him on the roof of the palace, looking over his kingdom and saying, "Is not this great Babylon, which I have built by my mighty power as a royal residence and for the glory of my majesty?" (Dan. 4:30). You probably know what happened next. God drove him out of his palace and reduced him to an animal, eating grass. Only then did this arrogant king bow to the majesty of the Lord, the greater King.

Why are all the details of this story preserved for us? I think that answer is both obvious and humbling. The story of Nebuchadnezzar has been retained for us because there is a bit of him in all of us. I wish I could stand apart from this story and say that I never do or say anything for my own glory, but I can't. Every act of disobedience, small or large, is motivated by self-glory. Every time you are impatient with someone, you are moved by self-glory. Every time you get mad because someone has disagreed with you, you are motivated by self-glory. Every time you yell at your kids because they have interrupted your evening, you are motivated by self-glory. When you amass material things rather than invest in God's kingdom work, you are motivated by self-glory. Every time you tell a story to bring attention to yourself, you are moved by self-glory. Every time you take credit for what you couldn't have produced on your own, you are motivated by self-glory. Whenever you are envious of the blessing or success of another, you are envious because of self-glory. Whenever you treat others as vehicles of or obstacles in the way of your pleasure and comfort, you are moved by self-glory. Whenever you act in vengeance and not forgiveness, you are motivated by self-glory. Every word of gossip, condemnation, or curse is moved by self-glory. The spiritual root of every sin is self-glory.

Sin turns all of us into glory thieves. Created to live for the glory of God, we live for the glory of self. This is the great and horrible exchange that causes a legacy of untold damage and human suffering. Our biggest sin problem is not the evil outside of us. We don't need a change of location. What each and every one of us needs is a heart- and life-glory realignment. Humanity has a massive glory problem. It started with the act of self-glory in the garden of Eden and is solved only by the intervention of God's powerful rescuing grace. Because sin still lives in us, in every forum of our lives, we live in the tension of the battle between the glory of self and the glory of God. The more you are aware of this battle, the more you will see it operating in your life.

By God's plan, corporate worship meets us in the midst of the battle, reminding us over and over again that the only glory worth living for is the glorious glory of God. Only this glory will produce in us and through us a harvest of eternal good. Self-glory never produces lasting peace. Self-glory never produces lasting contentment and joy. Self-glory never causes you to give yourself in self-sacrificing love. Self-glory never produces forgiveness and reconciliation. Self-glory never causes you to be patient, tender-hearted, and generous. Self-glory never causes you to turn from your sin and joyfully surrender to the will of the one who made you. Self-glory brings death, but living for the glory of God bursts with new life. There is no more beautiful way to live than to live for the glory of God. So we need his glory paraded before us over and over again in the gathering of his people. And we will continue to need it until we are on the other side and the great and destructive glory-war has forever ended.

———

Scripture: 1 Chronicles 16:28–30, Psalm 115:1, and Ephesians 3:21

Reflections: Do you allow the warnings in Scripture to help you see your sin more clearly? In what ways have you experienced the grace of God's patience?

Family Discussion: Discuss the statement "The spiritual root of every sin is self-glory."

Sunday 30

Corporate worship is designed to hold before us
the glorious glory of God so that self-glory would
not have the power to capture our hearts.

GOD IS THE DEFINITION OF GLORY. He is glorious all of the time and in every way. Glory is not one of his characteristics; it is the sum of all of his characteristics. He is glorious in power, sovereignty, wisdom, and love. He is glorious in mercy, patience, and forgiveness. He is glorious in holiness, faithfulness, and grace. He is the glorious Creator and sustainer of all things. He is a glorious Judge and Redeemer. He is the glorious conqueror of sin and death. His will for his creatures is glorious in every way. There is nothing inglorious in him, from him, or about him. His glory is gloriously glorious.

We were made to recognize that God is not like us. We were designed to be in awe of his glory. Our lives were meant to be shaped not by a pursuit of our own glory, but by the worship of his. A profoundly redemptive fear of the infinite gap between what God is like and what we are like is meant to humble us and drive us to him in confession, submission, and worship. As long as our own glory has more power in our hearts than the glory of God, we haven't yet understood what true glory is. So many of us live glory-deceived lives, living more in awe of ourselves than of God. As we live this way, we fail to see the glory displays that are all around us all the time and, because we do, we fail to recognize that the one who made and sustains all of these glories could not possibly be at all like us.

I wrote the following to remind us that God is not like us.

God isn't like us.
He never struggles like us,
never tires like us,
never fears like us,
never gets confused like us.
God isn't like us.
He has no past like us,
he has no future like us,
never hopes like us,
never fails like us,
never breaks a promise like us.
God isn't like us.
He never regrets like us,
never wonders if he could like us,
never doubts his plan like us,
never contradicts himself like us,
never chooses evil over good like us.
God is not like us.
He never attempts, but is unable like us,
never lives and dies like us,

never sins and covers like us,
never fails to love like us,
never acts selfishly like us.
God isn't like us.
He rules unchallenged, unlike us.
He is perfectly holy, unlike us.
He is always faithful, unlike us.
He abounds in love, unlike us.
He defines compassion, unlike us.
God isn't like us.
Eternal
Infinite
Self-sufficient
Omniscient
Omnipresent
Almighty
Full of grace and truth
Righteous in every way
Holy in anger
Pure in justice
Generous in mercy
Friend of sinners
Long-suffering
Ever patient
Infinite in power, tender of heart
Fount of forgiveness
Hope of the world
Creator
Sovereign
Savior

King of kings
Aren't you glad God is not like us?

Because, in the press of life, we can fail to see and live in awe
of the awesome glory of our Creator Savior King, we gather, week
after week, month after month, and year after year, to remember
and to celebrate that God is not like us. To know and believe this
will progressively change you, how you live your life, and your hope
for the future. May his glory continue to overwhelm and defeat
any vestiges of self-glory that still live inside of us, and may the
gatherings of his church stimulate and deepen our awe.

———

Scripture: 1 Samuel 2:2

Reflections: How might you and the way you live your life be
changed as you remember and celebrate that God is not like us?

Family Discussion: What are some of the *glory displays* that are all
around us all the time?

Sunday 31

Corporate worship is designed to remind you
of your identity in Christ so you won't waste
your time looking for identity elsewhere.

NOAH WAS LOST. He was beside himself and didn't know what
to do. For a while he hid his situation from his family, went
about his normal routine, and acted like everything was okay.
But things weren't okay, and neither was he. He had lost the one
thing that had given him meaning and purpose and, when it was
taken away from him, it felt as if life had been taken from him as
well. He had been raised in a wealthy, business-oriented, and successful family. He was determined to be successful too. Business
success was his identity. It was what made him feel worthwhile.
It was what got him up in the morning and what kept him going
throughout the day. It made him feel good and proud, worthy of
respect and appreciation. He knew who he was and what he was
meant to do, until it was all taken away. He had not only lost
his career, but he had lost himself. He woke up one day with no

career and no success. He didn't know who he was and what he was supposed to do. He lay in bed, lost.

———

Luke was sixteen years old, lying on a football field with a horribly contorted leg. His heart pounded so loudly that he could barely hear the people around him. His mind raced as they put him on a stretcher and lifted him into an ambulance. The next day, as he came to consciousness after his surgery and looked at the huge cast on his leg, he mumbled to himself, "Sixteen years old, and my life is already over." From about the time he could walk, he had been obsessed with sports. It was all he had ever wanted to do, and he was good at it. The dream was that he would become a professional athlete, have a stellar career, and be inducted into the hall of fame. He had been a coach's dream, a self-motivated, hard-working team player. But it all came to a screeching halt on that field behind his high school. He was hurt and angry, and he descended into an emotional and spiritual spiral that shocked and concerned everyone who knew him. Sports had been his identity. He was lost and didn't know what to do.

———

Chloe was a romantic. She was so captured by the dream of being married that as a little girl she kept a scrapbook of wedding dresses she cut from magazines. She dreamed not just of a wonderful wedding day and an exotic honeymoon, but also of a twenty-fifth and a fiftieth wedding anniversary. She saw herself as a wife and a mom. She knew she was destined to live in a lifelong love relationship, with children and wonderful vacations and holiday celebrations. After college, she loved her brief career, but she was convinced that was not who she was or what she was destined to do. She found a man, experienced his love, had the wonderful wedding, and began a life with him. But a car accident took it all away. She sat in her home, alone. There would be no children to share together and no long life of love. In that accident, she didn't just lose her young husband; she lost herself. Sitting that night all alone, she didn't know who she was or what to do. She was lost.

———

God designed us to be interpreters, meaning-makers. We want to know and to understand. So we never leave our lives alone. We are always turning our lives over and inside out, and we are always analyzing things to see what they're about. A significant part of making sense out of life is identity. We want to know who we are and what it is we are meant to be doing. Very early, in ways we aren't really conscious of, we begin to assign to ourselves an identity or identities. In and of itself this is not wrong to do. It's part of what it means to be rational. I have watched identity awareness develop quite naturally in my little granddaughters.

Here's what's important to understand: we weren't designed to get our primary identity horizontally. Vertical consciousness, that is, our awareness of God and our calling to live for him, was meant to be at the core of how we think about who we are and what we were made to do. From the earliest moments of Scripture, it is clear that God wanted Adam and Eve to think of themselves and their lives in connection to him. They were his creatures, created for a loving relationship with him and created to do his will. And when Adam and Eve decided to live independently, to step over God's prescribed boundaries and do what was forbidden, what was left was to look for identity somewhere other than at the feet of their Creator.

Ever since then, human beings have been looking to find their identity, their purpose, and their wholeness of heart in something in the creation, rather than in the Creator. So Jesus came not only to restore us to God, but to restore in us a true sense of self. He came so that once again we would find ourselves in union with him.

Peter addresses the gift of our union to Christ and the wealth of identity, meaning, and purpose that flow from it. In his first epistle, Peter is writing to people who, as believers, are suffering misunderstanding and mistreatment. Before he tells them that God designed them to live as aliens in a spiritually foreign world, he wants them to know who they are as the children of God. I encourage you to slowly read through 1 Peter, looking for identity statements. Let me give you one example: "But you are a chosen race, a royal priesthood, a holy nation, a people for his own possession, that you may proclaim the excellencies of him who called you out of darkness into his marvelous light. Once you were not a people, but now you are God's people; once you had not received mercy, but now you have received mercy" (1 Pet. 2:9–10).

I am so thankful for who I am as a child of God and that nothing can take this identity away from me. And I am thankful that throughout my life the worship gathering of God's children has held my union with Christ in front of me. I cannot be reminded enough that I am in him and he is in me, that I am deeply more than my job, my friendships, my family, my possessions, or my success. The most important thing about me, the thing that defines me and motivates me to do what I do, is that I am eternally a child of God, by grace united to the Son. I am thankful that in song, instruction, and fellowship, I get reminded of this truth week after week after week as I gather together with my brothers and sisters in Christ.

———

Scripture: Romans 8:16–17

Reflections: What identity statement do you find in Romans 8:16–17?

Family Discussion: Discuss the danger of looking for identity somewhere other than in the Creator.

Sunday 32

Corporate worship gives us three points of focus: upward (the glory of God), inward (our sin and God's grace), and outward (commitment to the work of his kingdom).

THINK ABOUT THE LOVING brilliance of God's plan to give us his church and to bless us with its regular gatherings. I can't imagine what my walk with the Lord would be like were it not for his church. I think about myself as a boy, sitting right up front with my family at Toledo Gospel Tabernacle, taking notes in my wide-margin Bible as I listened to William Bryan preach. I think of the importance of my high school years at Westgate Chapel, again listening to sermon after sermon on Sunday after Sunday. I think of all the believers gathered in these churches, who were examples to me and who loved and prayed for me. I think of my college years, hunting for a "good" church, finally discovering First Presbyterian Church, where both the preaching and the college fellowship were rich. I have thought about my seminary years, attending St. Matthew's Reformed Episcopal Church with Luella and the rich liturgy that so blessed and rooted us during those years. And I've thought about Grace Fellowship Church. Grace was not only a blessing after seminary, with its solid gospel preaching and warm familial fellowship, but it also became the church that launched me into this wonderful ministry life that I have been blessed to have.

I am deeply aware that God has blessed me with the church of Jesus Christ as a dominant spiritual influence in every epoch of my life. I am grateful that participating in the weekly gathering of the church was never a hard decision for me, because it was a habit formed in me as a child. I am blessed to say that my childhood, my youth, my marriage, and my ministry journey as an adult have all been formed and guided by the church. Because of the church, I have portion after portion of Scripture cemented in my memory. Because of the church, I learned the theology of God's word while still very young. Because of the church, I have hundreds of rich hymns of the faith committed to memory. Because of the church, I have been instructed, encouraged, warned, comforted, confronted, counseled, loved, guided, and cared for. Because my mom and dad took me to church Sunday after Sunday, I learned about the Lord and came to know and follow him. God used the life of the church to give me spiritual life. I love that I grew up and remain in the church and, each Sunday as we head to yet another gathering, I am aware that I need God's gift of his church now as much as I have ever needed it.

It's hard to communicate the enormity of the impact of the church on my life and just as impossible to calculate the value of having the habit of participating in its regular gatherings cemented into my life so young. These gatherings have not only set the rhythms for every week of my life, but they have established the rhythm of my spiritual life, my marriage, my parenting, my friendships, how I make decisions, and the course of my ministry.

Everything I do in ministry is born out of my love for and commitment to the local church. Everything I do in ministry is done to bless the church with deep gospel understanding and more gospel resources. I tell people all the time that my heart is in the local church.

As I ponder the influence of the church and why I am so committed to its gathering and its ministry, I realize that the church has given me three profound points of focus. These points of focus are not just biblical truths to think about, but are callings and life commitments that have given me tracks to run on, no matter my age, where I happen to live, and what I am called to do.

The Upward Focus of Corporate Worship. Corporate worship has helped me to keep the most important thing in life the most important thing in my life. Nothing is more important in life than to recognize and live in light of the existence, presence, power, rule, and glory of God. Wired deep into the design of every human being is the need to live in relationship with and willing submission to God. Not doing so is not just a loss of spirituality, but also a loss of my humanity. Every human being was meant to live a God-focused life. I confess that in the midst of a busy week or in times of physical or emotional hardship, God is not always at the center of my thoughts or the motivation of my heart. So I need his presence and glory put before me again and again. I love leaving a service of corporate worship with my mind and heart filled with the glory of the one who is the reason I was given life and breath.

The Inward Focus of Corporate Worship. Second only to the importance of knowing God is knowing yourself. Because we are all naturally self-righteous, because sin is deceitful, and because we often are more concerned about the wrongs of others' lives than we are our own, we need a mirror put before us again and again that helps us see ourselves with accuracy. Corporate worship not only puts God's glory in front of you, but it also reminds you again and again of how much you need his grace. In pointing to the unblemished holiness of God, corporate worship exposes how far away you and I are from being like him. Corporate worship is designed to expose us, convict us, and lead us to God's throne of grace where forgiveness and transforming power are to be found. I need these gatherings to show me both my need and where to find help.

The Outward Focus of Corporate Worship. God has designed corporate worship not just to expose my need of help, but to remind me over and over again that I have been called to be one of God's helpers. We need to be reminded that we are not just the recipients of God's amazing grace, but have been drafted by him to be instruments of that grace in the lives of others. We are not just sons and daughters of the King; we are his ambassadors, called to represent his character, his message, and his methods wherever he has placed us.

I have not outgrown my need for the upward, inward, and outward focus of the corporate gatherings of God's people, and I am sure that you haven't either.

———

Scripture: Psalm 100

Reflections: How do the three points of focus mentioned above help you to appreciate the importance of corporate worship?

Family Discussion: Discuss the importance of both living in relationship with God and having an accurate view of yourself.

Sunday 33

*Corporate worship is designed to remind us
that the greatest pandemic ever is the disease
of sin, and the only cure is found in the person
and work of the great physician, Jesus.*

IF YOU UNDERSTAND the historical and cultural setting, the
account of Jesus healing a leper is one of the most shocking
and encouraging stories in the New Testament. It confronts
us with who we are and who Jesus is. It is meant to leave us
both humbled and amazed. It powerfully exposes human need
and divine glory in just a few verses. We find the story early in
Mark's Gospel, which was written to demonstrate that Jesus of
Nazareth really is the Messiah, the Son of God. Mark's Gospel
is fast-paced and hard-hitting. Unlike Luke, Mark doesn't make
too many editorial comments. He puts the character, power,
passion, and plan of Jesus before us in such powerful ways that
it becomes more and more difficult, as you work through his
Gospel, to deny who he is. Early in Mark this story jumps off
the page:

And a leper came to him, imploring him, and kneeling said to him, "If you will, you can make me clean." Moved with pity, he stretched out his hand and touched him and said to him, "I will; be clean." And immediately the leprosy left him, and he was made clean. (Mark 1:40–42)

You can't really understand the radical wonder of this little vignette in the life and ministry of Jesus unless you understand the disease of leprosy. Leprosy is the name for a collection of infectious skin diseases. In New Testament times, people with leprosy would have lesions and infected scabs all over their skin. Sometimes, depending on the severity of the disease, the sufferer would lose fingers, an ear, or even his nose. In New Testament culture, leprosy was a thing to be feared, and lepers were shunned and despised. They were required to live separate not only from their family but from all of society. There was no known cure for this horrible disease.

So it is remarkable that this diseased outcast found his way to Jesus. It was an act of faith, desperation, and courage for him to push his way through whatever crowd was around Jesus and stand so close to him that Jesus could reach out and touch him. The unnamed leper obviously had heard about Jesus and his power and knew that he had no other hope but that this Jesus would heal him. His act of countercultural courage demonstrated his acknowledgment of the desperate nature of his condition. He had been afflicted with something neither he nor any other human being had the ability to cure. Jesus was his only hope.

The leper knew that Jesus had the power to heal him, which is why he said, "If you will." Convinced of the power of Jesus, he pleaded for Jesus to be willing. What happened next is hard to capture with the limitations of human language. Whenever lepers were near others, they would have to cry out, "Unclean, unclean," so that people would move away and not touch them. Touching a leper was considered a sentence to untold suffering and maybe even death. But Jesus is Lord Creator, and he was not afraid. He didn't just speak healing into this man. He reached out and did the unthinkable—he touched him. When I read this story, I imagine the gasps of the crowd: "Why would he do such a thing? Why is he not afraid to touch him?" But Jesus, the Messiah sent from heaven, was able to touch the untouchable and not be infected by the disease. As he touched him, Jesus announced his willingness and commanded the disease to leave this man.

The results were immediate. No need for medication to take effect. No need for therapy. No need for follow-up visits. This man, when touched by the Messiah, was immediately and completely healed of what was considered to be an incurable disease. Whether he knew it or not, he had encountered the Lord of creation. The physical world bowed to his command. Yes, it really is true, this Jesus of Nazareth is the God-man, the Messiah, the one sent by God to undo the damage that sin has done.

As you read the accounts of Christ's miracles, it's important to understand that each miracle is recorded to reveal the identity and glory of Jesus and to preach to us the gospel. It's important to ask why this little story of Jesus and the leper was preserved for us. Here you have a powerful physical picture of sin and redemption. Sin is the ultimate leprosy. It causes untold suffering and always leads to death. Sin is the incurable disease that infects everyone who has ever taken a breath. The disease of sin separates us from God and from one another. It leaves us lame and alone, unable to be what we were created to be and to do what we were created to do. Yet, spiritually diseased as we are, we are often all too skilled at convincing ourselves that we are spiritually healthy. When we look at ourselves, we don't see our sin-scarred condition, so we don't run after the touch of the great physician.

This account is in Mark's Gospel because we are that leper. From birth we are infected by sin, and only one has both the power and the willingness to help us. What difference would it make if Jesus was willing, but lacked the power? But our Savior is both tender in heart and awesome in power. He can cure of us of the ultimate disease, and he is willing.

Don't minimize your sin, don't separate yourself in shame, and don't mutter to yourself or others, "Unclean, unclean." Know that corporate worship is a lepers' gathering. We come again and again, confessing that there is evidence that our sickness has not been totally eradicated. We come again and again to celebrate that we have been touched by the Savior's healing hands, and we come to plead that he would touch us again and again until we are finally and eternally healed. Bring your disease to the Savior; he alone holds the cure.

———

Scripture: Luke 5:27–32

Reflections: Who in Luke 5:27–32 had convinced themselves they were spiritually healthy? How can you keep from being blinded by sin?

Family Discussion: Discuss why it is so crucial that our Savior be both tender in heart and awesome in power.

Sunday 34

*Corporate worship is designed to remind you
not to be captured by the things of this earth,
but to continue to seek the things that are above;
there is grace upon grace for this struggle.*

Maintaining the best lawn in the neighborhood.
Securing a great vacation spot.
Feeding the dog.
Shopping for a new car.
Paying the bills.
Streaming the next season of _____.
Carving out time for exercise.
Planning what the family is going to eat.
Achieving endless career goals.
Deciding what to do about the upcoming school year.
Planning for the holidays.
Navigating the distractions of university dorm life.
Watching the finals.
Remodeling the bathroom.

Wrapping the birthday gifts.
Tackling the piles of laundry.
Shopping for summer clothes.
Finding time to hit Starbucks.
Searching for a new apartment.

The needs, desires, commitments, and distractions of life are endless. It's not that all of the earthly things that occupy our minds and our time are bad. Many of them are good and necessary, the unavoidable responsibilities of life. We are physical people, living in a physical world, so there are a host of physical things that need to be maintained. God designed us to live in community with one another, so there are relationships that need attention so they remain healthy, unified, and loving. God designed us to work, so labor consumes a big chunk of our time, attention, and effort. God created us to go through seasons of life, and each season has its own responsibilities and challenges. There is busyness that is the result of who God made us to be and what he designed for us to do. Busyness is not sinful in and of itself.

But it's important to understand that God also designed us to be treasure-oriented. We all look at life and decide what is important and what is not. Each of our lives is shaped by a set of values, even if we are not aware of them. You are willing to make sacrifices of time, energy, and money for what is valuable to you. Everyone lives for treasure of some kind. The thing that is your treasure will control your heart, and what has control of your heart will control your thoughts, desires, words, choices, and actions. This side of eternity, a war of treasure is fought in our hearts.

Another way Scripture talks about this is though the concept of *kingdoms*. We were made by God to be kingdom-oriented. As the children of God, we always have a foot in two kingdoms: the kingdom of this world and the kingdom of God. God has placed us in this world, and our existence here has meaning and purpose. But as the children of God, we are also citizens of a greater kingdom, the kingdom of God. At the level of our hearts, these two kingdoms are at war. Will our hearts be controlled by and will our lives be shaped by the kingdom of this world or the kingdom of God? This battle is exposed for us in 1 John 2:15–17:

> Do not love the world or the things in the world. If anyone loves the world, the love of the Father is not in him. For all that is in the world—the desires of the flesh and the desires of the eyes and pride of life¯is not from the Father but is from the world. And the world is passing away along with its desires, but whoever does the will of God abides forever.

Notice John's focus. His concern is not first about the busyness of your schedule. No, John's primary concern is for your heart. If your heart is controlled by a love for the things of this earth, then they will shape your hopes and dreams and dictate how you invest your time, energy, and resources. If you love your heavenly Father, you will seek his kingdom and his righteousness, and you will find your meaning and purpose not in the things of this earth but in the things above. If I could watch a video of your last six weeks, what would I conclude you truly love and value? What would I think you truly live for?

John reminds us of how foolish it is to be consumed by the things of this world. It takes John just five words to demonstrate how foolish it is to live for the kingdom of this world: "The world is passing away." But the kingdom of God lasts forever. We are either living for what will not last or for what is eternal. So it's not sinful to be busy, but we must examine the values behind our busyness. Here's where God's plan for his church to regularly gather is so incredibly helpful. This gathering provides us with regular values-clarification as it puts before us the comforts and callings of the kingdom of God and as it displays for us the glories of our risen Savior King. In so doing it calls us again and again not to set our hearts on the things of this earth but on the things that are above, and it reminds us that we do not fight this battle alone. By grace, the King meets us in our everyday war and battles on our behalf. We need that good news again and again.

———

Scripture: Matthew 13:44–46

Reflections: What do you treasure? That is, what are you willing to make the sacrifices of time, energy, and money for? Do you need to rethink where you find meaning and purpose? How can gathering with God's people help you to do this?

Family Discussion: Talk about why it is foolish to live for the kingdom of this world.

Sunday 35

*Corporate worship is designed to remind you
that the most valuable thing in your life is
something you could have never earned or
deserved. It was and is a gift of divine grace.*

MY FATHER WAS a very hard worker. He worked a full-time job
and had two businesses that he operated out of our home. He was
the first one up in the morning and the last one to go to bed at
night. He believed in the Protestant work ethic, and he instilled
in his children a belief in the dignity of work. He did not believe
that work was a curse, but rather that human beings were designed
to work. For him, working well and working hard was a way to
express the dignity of one's humanity. As my sophomore year of
high school was drawing to a close, my dad sat me down and told
me I had to find a job. He told me that on the very first day of
summer break I was to put on a suit and go look for work. He said
I had to leave at nine o'clock and keep looking until five o'clock
and that I should do that every day until I got a job. I knew he was
serious, so I headed over to the local mall and applied for a job as

a stock boy at JCPenney. I was hired immediately, and I worked that job until I graduated from high school.

I am thankful that I learned early the value of being willing to work. In college, at seminary, and in my doctoral work, what Dad instilled in me served me well. I have never found it hard to work, and I have never needed a boss to stand over me to assure that I work. Most of us have learned that many of the good things in life come as a result of work. We've worked our way through our schooling. We've worked our way from job to job. We've worked to have a decent place to live and to keep it maintained. We've worked so that we can afford the things we need. We've worked so that we can enjoy the occasional vacation away from work. We've worked to keep ourselves healthy. We've pulled weeds, cut trees, turned over soil, planted grass and flowers, trimmed bushes, and mowed lawns in order to make our surroundings beautiful. We've built things, restored things, and painted things. We've cooked ten thousand meals and washed more dishes than we would like to recount. We've washed, ironed, and mended clothes. We've made endless beds and vacuumed miles of carpet. Work is the inescapable calling of people made in the image of God. You cannot have a healthy or success-ful life devoid of a commitment to work. We were made to work, and all of us have to do it in some way, whether we want to or not.

So it would make sense to approach our relationship with God with a "work hard and you'll get what's good" mentality. It would make sense for us to fall into thinking that hardworking people get God's blessing and lazy people don't. It would make sense to approach God thinking that we have to earn his favor and purchase his love by our effort. When it comes to a relationship with God, it would make sense to think "do good, get good." But with God all the rules are different. With him the best work ethic always falls miserably short.

With God we are confronted with the truth that no hard work can ever earn you a relationship with him. I am thankful for my dad's instruction and example when it comes to work, but I've had to learn that I cannot work my way to God. Here is why our work will never earn us God's favor.

The standard is too high. It's easy to state God's standard: absolute perfection. This is what it would take to gain acceptance with God. For fallen human beings, it's like we're being asked to stand in the middle of a gymnasium and jump and touch the ceiling. You could jump for a thousand years and never get remotely close. All you would end up with are exhausted legs and diminished hope. God's standard is unreachable. Total perfection is humanly unattainable. When it comes to his law, a spotless record of obedience is beyond everyone's reach. In the face of this standard, we all stand condemned.

Sin has left us too weak. It is the damage of sin that makes us fall short of God's glorious standard (see Rom. 3). We entered the world weak and unable. This is what the doctrine of total depravity explains. It's not that we are as bad as we can be, but rather that the damage of sin reaches to every part of our personhood. We don't love as we should, think as we should, desire what we should, speak as we should, choose what we should, act as we should, worship who we should, and so on. Apart from God's grace, everything we do and say, crave and pursue, or plan and purpose is in some way tainted by sin. Sin leaves us both unwilling and unable.

Our blindness is too deep. Sin leaves us blind to who we are, who God is, what life is truly about, and what it is that we need. So no one, apart from grace, really understands or seeks God. The average person walking down the street isn't crying out for God. If you have a hunger for God, you know you have been visited by his grace. Our spiritual blindness is so pervasive that we are blind even to our blindness. Thinking we are wise, capable, and righteous, we are in truth blind and unable to see the truth apart from grace.

We need a substitute. In our weakness and blindness, we were without hope and without God in this world. There was only one hope for us. We needed a substitute, one who could stand in our place and do on our behalf what we could never do: live a perfectly righteous life, die a substitutionary death, and rise again in the ultimate victory over sin and death. So, in a move of glorious grace, God sent his Son as the second Adam. He was victorious where Adam failed, so that we might be forgiven and adopted into God's family.

So we gather to remember that when it comes to acceptance and relationship with God, our very best efforts, our hardest and most faithful work, fall short. We have only one hope: grace. And we gather to remember that grace is a person, and his name is Jesus. There is no grace apart from the person and work of Jesus. We don't have to measure up, because he perfectly measured up to God's standard on our behalf. We are eternally forgiven and accepted not because of our work, but because of the work he did for us in the grace of his life, death, and resurrection. So we joyfully gather to remember and celebrate the Sabbath of rest that is ours in Jesus.

———

Scripture: John 6:27–29

Reflections: Are you thankful or disappointed that hard work can never earn a relationship with God?

Family Discussion: Discuss the value of hard work and why we cannot work our way to God.

Sunday 36

*Corporate worship is designed to hold before
you the unstoppable grace that is your hope
for today and for all the days to come.*

"WE ARE GOING TO HAVE TO DO SURGERY." I've heard these
words ten times over the last seven years. It has been very hard.
It seems that, just as my body begins to recover, I'm told another
surgery is necessary. I have had to learn how to deal with pain, but
without relying on highly addictive medications. I have had to accept chronic weakness that seems to leave me with barely half of a
day to do the work I am so privileged to do. I have had to accept
that I will be sick in some way for the rest of my life. I have had to
resist asking questions that have no answers and not allow myself
to go down the rabbit hole of "what ifs." In some ways I am still
very fit, but the damage to my body is inescapable.

On one hand I am not surprised that I have faced physical
hardship. I know that I live in a broken and groaning world where
suffering is a universal experience. I knew that this brokenness
would enter my door somehow, sometime, and in some way. I know

that being a child of God doesn't give me a ticket out of suffering. I know it is God's choice for me to live between the "already" and the "not yet" in a fallen world that is not operating as he intended. I know there are many whose suffering has been way more severe and long term than mine. I know I have been blessed to be surrounded by people who love me, and I know I have been given excellent medical care. But it would be dishonest for me to say that these years have been easy.

I have come to understand that you never suffer passively, because you never come to your suffering neutrally. There are significant things that we always drag into our suffering. We come to these hard moments with views of God, perspectives on life, assessments about our identity, thoughts on what we deserve or don't deserve, a set of values, and a catalog of personal hopes and dreams. These together comprise a functional theology that structures the way we suffer. In suffering, it is vital to understand that you don't just suffer the thing that you are suffering; you also suffer *the way* you are suffering. We all don't suffer the same, because we all don't bring the same things to our suffering.

If you bring doubts about God into your moments of suffering, it makes sense that you would run away from him and not to him. If you have allowed yourself to question God's goodness, faithfulness, and love, then it makes sense that in times of suffering you would bring God into the court of your judgment and question his character and care. If you have struggled with looking over the fence at someone else's life, wondering why he got what you crave, then it makes sense that you would struggle deeply with why your life is hard and others' seem so easy. If you've tended to struggle with guilt, then it makes sense that you would conclude that this moment of suffering is punishment for your past sins. The point is that the things we bring into our suffering really do powerfully affect the way that we suffer.

I am deeply grateful for one thing I brought into my suffering that has made this burden infinitely lighter to bear. I came to these years of physical travail completely persuaded that God's grace is unstoppable. Now, this doesn't make me some kind of spiritual hero. Being fully persuaded of the constant presence and operation of God's grace is a testament to my years in the church. It is the legacy of thousands of worship services, thousands of sermons, hundreds and hundreds of small group Bible studies, and thousands of words of counsel, confrontation, and comfort from brothers and sisters in Christ. The fact that we will all suffer in some way in this broken world is a powerful argument for the essentiality of the church of Jesus Christ and its regular gatherings. The church planted in me seeds of assurance of the constant presence and power of God's grace. These seeds have grown into an oak tree of assurance that stands with strength in my heart.

So, on my hardest days, I did not feel forsaken by God. I did not think I was being punished for my sin. I did not think that his promises no longer applied. I did not think that his grace had lost its power. And I did not think that God had withdrawn his love for me. On many occasions over the last seven years I have thanked God for the powerful impact of the church on me. I am very aware and thankful that a legacy of Sundays shapes the way I suffer.

One particular passage reminds me that God's rescuing, forgiving, transforming, empowering, and delivering grace is unstoppable, even though it doesn't mention the word *grace*. This passage has been a faithful and encouraging friend to me:

> Who shall bring any charge against God's elect? It is God who justifies. Who is to condemn? Christ Jesus is the one who died—more than that, who was raised—who is at the right hand of God, who indeed is interceding for us. Who shall separate us from the love

of Christ? Shall tribulation, or distress, or persecution, or famine, or nakedness, or danger, or sword? As it is written,

> "For your sake we are being killed all the day long;
> we are regarded as sheep to be slaughtered."

No, in all these things we are more than conquerors through him who loved us. For I am sure that neither death nor life, nor angels nor rulers, nor things present nor things to come, nor powers, nor height nor depth, nor anything else in all creation, will be able to separate us from the love of God in Christ Jesus our Lord. (Rom. 8:33–39)

Corporate worship is one of God's tools in preparing us for hardships to come; he uses it to convince us of his perfect goodness and his ever-present and all-powerful grace. And he uses it to remind us that this grace does its best work when we are weak.

———

Scripture: 2 Corinthians 12:9–10 and 1 Peter 4:1–2

Reflections: What thoughts do you bring into your times of suffering?

Family Discussion: Discuss how knowing God's perfect goodness and all–powerful grace can prepare us for hardship, and comfort us in moments of suffering.

Sunday 37

Corporate worship is designed to alert us to the fact that life is spiritual war and to arm us for that war with the weapons of the gospel.

Finally, be strong in the Lord and in the strength of his might. Put on the whole armor of God, that you may be able to stand against the schemes of the devil. For we do not wrestle against flesh and blood, but against the rulers, against the authorities, against the cosmic powers over this present darkness, against the spiritual forces of evil in the heavenly places. Therefore take up the whole armor of God, that you may be able to withstand in the evil day, and having done all, to stand firm. Stand therefore, having fastened on the belt of truth, and having put on the breastplate of righteousness, and, as shoes for your feet, having put on the readiness given by the gospel of peace. In all circumstances take up the shield of faith, with which you can extinguish all the flaming darts of the evil one; and take the helmet of salvation, and the sword of the Spirit, which is the word of God, praying at all times in the Spirit, with all prayer and supplication. To that end, keep alert with all perseverance, making supplication for all the saints, and also for me, that words may be given to me in opening my mouth boldly to proclaim the mystery of the gospel, for which I am an ambassador in chains, that I may declare it boldly, as I ought to speak. (Eph. 6:10–20)

To get the full power, intent, necessity, and practicality of these words, which come at the close of the book of Ephesians, you have to pay attention to the flow of Paul's letter. In chapters 1–3, Paul paints a majestic portrait of the gospel of Jesus Christ. In chapters 4 through the beginning of 6, he details what it means to live, in every area of your life, in light of the gospel. For Paul, the gospel is not only the message of salvation in Jesus Christ, but it is also a lens through which we can look at everything in our lives and a guide for how to act, react, and respond in every dimension of our lives. In the midst of applying the gospel to the things we deal with every day, Paul suddenly begins to talk about spiritual warfare and arming ourselves for war. At first look, it may seem as if Paul is changing the subject, but he isn't. This discussion of spiritual war is the best possible summary for all the practical applications of the gospel he has made in chapters 4 and 5. He wants his readers to know that every domain of human life is a place of spiritual war. The great war between good and evil, the great war that takes place in our hearts, the great war between God's way and our way, the great war between the kingdom of God and the kingdom of this world, and the great war between light and darkness takes place in the ordinary situations, locations, and relationships of our everyday lives. It is helpful to know that marriage is spiritual war. The great conflict in marriage is not first between husbands and wives but against "spiritual forces of evil." The big battle of parenting is not the battle to get your kids to obey, but rather standing strong against the "schemes of the devil" and his work to divide and destroy. The raging battle in your world of talk is not about getting your point across; it's a spiritual war for the heart that is behind your words.

It is enormously helpful to know that we don't "wrestle against flesh and blood." That means the big enemy is not your spouse, your children, your parents, your neighbor, your boss, or your friend. We have one big enemy, and spiritual health in all of these relationships is found when we're defending ourselves against him. He is a tempter, seeking to lure us into living for ourselves rather than surrendering to the will and way of our Lord. He is a deceiver, seeking to bring us to a point where we doubt God's wisdom, goodness, and love. He works to make us believe that our sin is not so sinful and that we don't really need God's help after all. He works to stir up our anger, to diminish our hope, and to build our pride. And he does all of this in the houses, workplaces, and cars of daily life. This means that this great spiritual war is not some weird demon-and-deliverance exception to the normal Christian life. No, Paul wants us to know that between the "already" of our conversion and the "not yet" of our homegoing, spiritual warfare is a regular, normal part of a Christian's life.

But we don't have to live in fear and we don't have to give up hope, because God, in the goodness of his wisdom and love, arms his children for the battle. The question is, Have we taken up the armament he has given us? It's naïve to think that somehow, some-way this battle will elude us. It's foolish to think that we will avoid this war in our marriage, parenting, friendships, job, or church. And it's irresponsible to not take Paul's warning and encouragement seriously. So I am thankful that, in the gathering of God's people for worship and instruction, I am again and again alerted to this war. I am thankful that in these times of corporate worship, I remember that I have been given weapons for the battle. And I am thankful that I am reminded again and again that I never fight this spiritual war alone or in my own power. God fights for me and will continue to fight for me until that fight is no longer needed. His Spirit now resides in me and battles for my heart even when I don't have the sense to engage in the battle myself. He does not grow weary of the fight. He never gets discouraged in the middle of the war. He never loses his zeal for the battle. He never walks away from his promises. He will continue to fight until that last enemy is under his feet. I have hope because the Lord of hosts is my captain and he will win. God has ordained that I gather with his people so that I can get to know him, trust him, follow him, and learn what it means to take up the weapons of war he has given me. I need the gatherings of his church because spiritual war is real, and it rages in all the places where I live, work, and play.

———

Scripture: 2 Corinthians 10:4–5

Reflections: How seriously do you take Paul's warning and encouragement from Ephesians 6? How can times of corporate worship help to prepare us for spiritual battle?

Family Discussion: Talk about why it is helpful to know that we don't "wrestle against flesh and blood."

Sunday 38

Corporate worship is designed to remind you that the Lord of goodness, glory, and grace is your Father. He is near, he receives your worship, and he hears your cries.

IT IS SO ENCOURAGING to know that the goodness of the Lord is *father* goodness.

> As a father shows compassion to his children,
>> so the LORD shows compassion to those who fear him.
>> (Ps. 103:13)

Pray then like this:

> "Our Father in heaven,
>> hallowed be your name." (Matt. 6:9)

Look at the birds of the air: they neither sow nor reap nor gather into barns, and yet your heavenly Father feeds them. Are you not of more value than they? (Matt. 6:26)

If you then, who are evil, know how to give good gifts to your children, how much more will your Father who is in heaven give good things to those who ask him! (Matt. 7:11)

And do not seek what you are to eat and what you are to drink, nor be worried. For all the nations of the world seek after these things, and your Father knows that you need them. Instead seek his kingdom, and these things will be added to you. Fear not, little flock, for it is your Father's good pleasure to give you the kingdom. (Luke 12:29–32)

And I will be a father to you,
    and you shall be sons and daughters to me,
says the Lord Almighty. (2 Cor. 6:18)

Blessed be the God and Father of our Lord Jesus Christ, who has blessed us in Christ with every spiritual blessing in the heavenly places. (Eph. 1:3)

See what kind of love the Father has given to us, that we should be called children of God; and so we are. (1 John 3:1)

The word picture of a father in these passages is so evocative and beautiful. Yes, God is the Creator, the Almighty One, the sovereign King, the Lord of hosts, the sacrificial Lamb, and the victorious Redeemer. But it is essential to understand that:

The Creator is your Father.
The Almighty One is your Father.
The sovereign King is your Father.

The Lord of hosts is your Father.
The victorious Redeemer is your Father.

In the magnificence of his glory, God is a Father to all who put their trust in him. He is not a distant King. He is not separate from his creation. He doesn't just rule us; he also loves us with the compassion of a Father. You wake up every morning to a Father who is not just your King, but he is a King who exercises his rule over all things for your good because you are one of his children.

As an earthly father, I want what is best for my children, and I want to do what is best for them, but I am far less than perfect. When they were young, I would get irritated with them. I would get discouraged. I would grow tired and weary. I would not always have the best attitude or speak the right words. Sometimes I misjudged them. Sometimes I was too harsh and not forgiving enough. I often failed to model for them what it looks like to trust in the Lord. I failed my children in many ways. But I loved them dearly, thought about them constantly, did all I could to be patient and provide for them, and told them I loved them ten thousand times.

My children did experience my father goodness, but it was imperfect, weak, and failing. But God is not like me. He is the perfect Father. He is always faithful, always patient, always kind, always forgiving, and always willing to exercise his power for the good of his children. And he does all of these things without any failure of any kind. Peace of heart and life is really found in resting in the perfectly faithful and loving fatherly care of the Lord. I do not have to worry, because he knows just what I need. I do not have to fear his anger, because he disciplines me as a loving Father. I do not have to control everything in my life, because he rules for my benefit with the compassion of my Father.

Anxiety builds as I forget him and attempt to bear the load of life on my all too small shoulders. So I need the gathering of the church to remind me over and over again that, because of grace, I live in the arms of the one and only completely holy and perfectly loving Father. I am the object of his compassion not because I deserve it, but because he has chosen me to be one of his children. This is the best of news. Why would I not want to hear it again and again?

———

Scripture: 1 Corinthians 1:3, Mark 11:25, and Luke 6:36

Reflections: Ponder the significance of having the Almighty Creator Redeemer as your *Father*. What difference would it make in your daily life if you made that your first thought every morning?

Family Discussion: Talk about how being perfectly loved by your heavenly Father can give you peace of heart and life.

Sunday 39

Corporate worship is designed to fill you with a Christ-infused joy that no person, situation, or disappointment has the power to take away.

IT'S SAD TO WATCH someone continually look for something where it simply can't be found. But we all do it. The deceptiveness of sin causes us to look horizontally for what will only ever be found vertically. We look to the creation to give us what only the Creator can. We try to turn people into little messiahs. We look to material things to supply spiritual needs. So we end up discouraged, disappointed, hurt, angry, sad, and without hope.

Everybody searches for joy, that deep experience of satisfaction, contentment, inner peace, and happiness. Some of us look to marriage to satiate our joy hunger. We dream that once we are married, we will experience real joy. But a marriage between two sinners will never deliver unbroken joy. Some of us look to material things. We tell ourselves that once we have that dream house, we'll be content. But if houses could satisfy our hearts, then the person and work of Jesus wouldn't have been necessary.

Some of us look to our careers, but the ebb and flow of a career gives us cause for worry and concern rather than unstoppable joy. Some of us look to physical health and beauty, but the body gets sick and marches toward the weariness and weakness of old age. Some of us try to entertain ourselves into some kind of numbing joy, but whatever buzz we get doesn't last. Some of us go from experience to experience, traveling the world and looking for fulfillment, but the happiness is short-lived and we're soon hunting for the next experience. Some of us look to ministry success, but that never delivers what we're searching for. Somehow, someway, everyone searches for joy and, sadly, most of us look for it in all the wrong places.

Even though many of us aren't aware of it, we're looking for joy that no person, no situation, and no disappointment can take away. True joy is never the result of external situations, locations, and relationships. True joy is a matter of the heart. True joy grows in the soil of gratitude. Even if you've never thought about it, you have experienced that this is true. You never go to grumbling and complaining people for joy, because you instinctively know they don't have any. The more you spend your day cataloging your complaints about things in your life, the less joy you have. The more you look over the fence and wish you had the life of someone else, the less joy you have. The more you feel ripped off, neglected, or forgotten, the less joy you have. The more your prayers are a list of complaints and wants, the less joy you have. The more you look at your life and calculate what is missing, rather than celebrating what you've been given, the less joy you have. The more you live in a world of "if onlys," the less joy you have. The more you doubt the presence, wisdom, goodness, and grace of God, the less joy you have. Joy doesn't grow well in the soil of bitterness or complaint.

But for believers, we have eternal reasons to experience joy, which nothing or no one can take away. Unshakable joy grows and matures in the soil of past, present, and future grace. I need constant reminders of that grace. I need to hear songs of grace, and I need to hear that grace expounded, explained, and applied. So I am thankful that God has given me the church. Let's look at the grace that is the soil in which a grateful and joyful heart grows.

Past grace. It is a wonderful thing not to be weighed down with past regrets that you can now do nothing whatsoever about. Since none of us are perfect, we all look back with regret at choices we made, actions we took, and words we said. I wish I had been a perfect, loving husband, but over the years I have failed so many times and in so many ways. I wish I could say the same about my relationship with my children. I wish I had always reflected Christ to them, but many times I fell short. I wish I had always spent my time and money wisely, but my idolatrous heart often got in the way. But I can look at my past with joy, because every single moment of my past sin, from the smallest to the most consequential, was nailed to the cross of Jesus Christ, and I bear them no more! I am further blessed because the one who forgives me is also a restorer. He brings healing, reconciliation, and restoration in places where sin has left things broken.

Present grace. I love how Peter talks about present grace. He says that we have already been given everything we need for life and godliness (2 Pet. 1:3). He is not talking primarily about eternal life here. You know this because he uses the word *godliness*. Godliness is a right-here, right-now word. Godliness is a God-honoring life between the time I come to know him and the time I go home to be with him forever. Peter is talking about a present supply of God's grace that is so completely rich that he can actually say that it gives me everything I need. No, he isn't talking about everything I want, but rather, all the things that I need to be what God designed me to be and to do what he calls me to do. I have it all! I am rich, rich, rich in grace. No spiritual need is ignored, and nothing necessary is unsupplied.

Future grace. Grace frees me from anxiety about the future. First, I know that all the things coming down the road, which are out of my hands, are under the wise and powerful control of my Lord. I know that he rules all of these things not only for his own glory but also for the sake of his children. But there is more. I know that my destiny is secure. Because of God's grace, I am heading to an eternity whose glory is so glorious that it is almost impossible for my mind to grasp. I will live forever with my Lord in a place where sin and suffering are no more and where peace and righteousness will reign forever and ever.

As we focus on the past, present, and future glories of God's grace, we begin to experience a depth of joy that the disappointments of life in this fallen world are unable to take away. God calls us to gather because he knows how forgetful and joyless we can be. He knows how important it is for us to gather, remember, and celebrate the amazing past, present, and future grace that he has so willingly poured down on us. We leave gathering after gathering with renewed gratitude in our hearts as we remember that we are the children of the Lord of grace and glory who is the only source of sturdy, unshakable joy.

———

Scripture: Psalm 16:11

Reflections: Why can you look upon your past with joy? Why can you look toward the future with confident joy?

Family Discussion: Talk about how you would define true joy. What are some obstacles to experiencing true joy?

Sunday 40

Corporate worship is designed to welcome God's hungry children to sit at his table once again and have our hungry hearts filled with what he alone can supply.

Hunger
moves,
activates,
drives
us all.
The little girl
prances into the room,
announcing to her mama,
"I'm hungry."
The old man,
tray on his lap,
unable to feed himself,
waits for assistance
as he mumbles to himself,
"I'm hungry."

The teenager,
alone in the school hallway,
craves for a companion,
watches packs of friends
walk by and thinks,
"I'm hungry."
The young MBA,
newly arrived in New York,
stands on a sidewalk
on Wall Street
and says to himself,
"I'm hungry."
The little boy,
temporarily lost
in the biggest toy store
he's ever been in,
looks wide-eyed
at the magical displays
and whispers,
"I'm hungry."
The rugged officer,
surveying the battlefield,
contemplating the rages of war,
longing for a final peace,
with a tired heart thinks,
"I'm hungry."
The expectant mother,
having lost children
before birth,

silently weeps in fear,
hoping for good news
and in her tears prays,
"I'm hungry."
The artist stares
at another finished canvas,
glances at too many
stacked against the studio wall,
longing for a gallery opportunity,
and with disappointment says,
"I'm hungry."
The patient sits in the oncology center,
another day, another infusion,
wearied by the struggle of disease,
too weak to hope for health,
her tears once again saying,
"I'm hungry."
Bills strewn across the table
depict expenses overwhelming income;
afraid to open another envelope,
frustration wells up within
as he says to himself,
"I'm hungry.
Single and middle-aged,
the dream of marriage
flickering and fading,
aloneness overwhelming,
she unlocks the empty apartment
and once again mumbles to no one,

"I'm hungry."
Humanity is a community
of the hungry:
hungry for food,
hungry for acceptance,
hungry for success,
hungry for peace,
hungry for hope,
hungry for home,
hungry for satisfaction,
hungry for rest,
hungry for safety,
hungry for a future,
hungry for love.
Our deepest hungers
are not physical;
they are deeply spiritual.
Our hearts growl
with hunger
for what was meant to be,
for how the world was designed to be,
for what we were created to be,
for rescue from what was not meant to be.
Our deeper hunger
is satisfied only at one table,
satiated only by one food,
craving only one banquet.
Deep in every human heart
is a hunger
for the Lord's table of grace,

where hungry souls
eat and are satisfied,
with no work of their own,
with no cost to them,
the meal paid for by their host
by the price of his life,
an expression of the extent
of his mercy.
So, when you are hungry,
wherever you are,
with others
or alone,
whatever you are hungry for,
remember that every human hunger
points you to a deeper hunger,
one satisfied only by your
Creator.
His satisfying table is open to you
only because of his grace.
His banquet is the one
soul-satisfying feast
that will never ever end.

So run again and run often to the table of the Lord. Eat and
drink of his goodness with your brothers and sisters. Be filled
and celebrate. Your invitation to the table has been paid for by
your Savior.

———

Scripture: Psalm 36:7–9, Matthew 5:6, and John 6:35

Reflections: What are you most hungry for? How can this hunger point you to Christ?

Family Discussion: Discuss the stunning reality of the statement "His banquet is the one soul-satisfying feast that will never end."

Sunday 41

*Corporate worship is designed to rescue us from
our gospel amnesia and root our identity once
again in the person and work of Jesus.*

AMNESIA IS A HORRIBLE and terrifying condition. It robs you of
your past, your identity, and your relationships, and in so doing it
robs you of your future. It can happen in an instant, but will steal
your lifetime. A brain disease or an accident might bring it on, but
suddenly the victim doesn't know who he is, he doesn't remember his life, and he recognizes none of his loved ones. He doesn't
know where he's been, what he's accomplished, what he knows
and believes, or who he loves and is loved by. How terrifying it
must be to live in this void. So much of how we make sense out of
life has to do with how we understand our past, how we interpret
our identity, and how we see ourselves in relation to others. Here
stands a rational person, but one who has been robbed of all the
tools that we normally use to make sense of our lives.

We look with pity at the poor amnesiac. But there is a form
of amnesia that inflicts many of us, though we are unaware of

our condition. In fact, I am deeply persuaded that God gave us the regular gatherings of his church as a defense against this life-altering amnesia. Sadly, many of us live in either a momentary or an extended state of gospel amnesia. In the busyness of life, in the hunger for success, in the joys and sorrows of family, or in the pursuit of personal hopes and dreams, we forget who we are and what we have been given in Christ. For some of us, this means that pride grows, as we take credit for what we could have never achieved or produced on our own. For others of us, we fall into living as if God doesn't exist, taking our lives into our own hands and writing our own rules. Some of us, forgetting that only God is worthy of our worship, allow our hearts to be increasingly captured by the things of this world. For some of us, forgetting gives worry, fear, and anxiety room to take root in our hearts. For others, we become lethargic, no longer motivated by the bright comforts and callings of the gospel.

The point is that gospel amnesia never goes anywhere good and never produces good in us and through us. So we need tools of defense against our spiritual amnesia. When it comes to the gospel, corporate worship is one of God's best anti-amnesia defenses. God never intended the gospel of Jesus Christ to be just an entrance and an exit. It is vastly more than just the means by which we are brought into relationship with God and the guarantee of an eternal future with him. Between your conversion and your passage into eternity, God intends the gospel to be the lens you look through to understand everything in your life as well as the guide for the way you live your life. The gospel is not just something you accept and believe, but it is the thing that forms the way you live in the situations, locations, and relationships of your life.

The gospel forms how you understand your identity.

The gospel patterns how you understand and behave in your marriage.

The gospel defines for you the task of parenting.

The gospel provides the basis for how you understand love and sexuality.

The gospel teaches you how to invest your time, energy, and money.

The gospel helps you understand how to steward your physical body.

The gospel helps you understand how to be a citizen.

The gospel defines for you what justice looks like.

The gospel tells you what it means to live in community with others.

The gospel holds out the imperative of participation in the life and ministry of the body of Christ.

The gospel enables you to properly interpret your past.

The gospel gives you hope for the future.

The gospel teaches you how to live in a world that doesn't function as God intended.

The gospel tells you what to love and what to hate.

The gospel exposes your heart while offering you God's forgiveness.

Right here, right now, it is impossible to be what God designed you to be and to do what he's called you to do without the glorious comfort and call of the gospel of Jesus Christ. It is impossible that you and I could overthink or overstudy the gospel message. We will never come to a place where we are gospel graduates. The well of the gospel is so deep that we will never reach the bottom. This is why the church—its worship, instruction, discipleship, and ministries—are absolutely essential for each one of us.

This everyday, life-shaping gospel awareness and focus is what animates the apostle Paul in Ephesians 4. Having beautifully explained the richness of what God has given us in his Son, the Lord Jesus, Paul wants his readers to know that this glorious message of redeeming grace is meant to shape the way they approach everything in their lives. The gospel of the grace of the Lord Jesus Christ is meant to be the ultimate game changer, the final life paradigm shift, so he says, "I therefore, a prisoner for the Lord, urge you to walk in a manner worthy of the calling to which you have been called, with all humility and gentleness, with patience, bearing with one another in love, eager to maintain the unity of the Spirit in the bond of peace" (Eph. 4:1–3). Essentially Paul is saying, "You know that wonderful call you have received to, by grace, become the children of God? That call ought to form the way you live." Never forget that call in the way you live in the church; never forget that call in your marriage; never forget that call in your parenting; never forget that call in your speech; never forget that call in the workplace; never forget that call as you use your money; never forget that call when you are angry; and never forget that call in moments of temptation. Do everything you can do to avoid a way of living that is the result of gospel amnesia.

So, with joy, we head to another gathering of the children of God, because we know how prone we are to forget and we know how good it is of God to give us this constant tool of defense against our spiritual amnesia tendencies.

———

Scripture: Colossians 1:9–11

Reflections: Why is it impossible to study or think upon the gospel message too much?

Family Discussion: Talk about how the gospel is so much more than simply a beginning and an end. How can corporate worship remind us to keep our gospel lenses on?

Sunday 42

Corporate worship is designed to keep your eyes
focused on the presence, promises, purposes,
and grace of your sovereign Savior King.

A FEW BLOCKS DOWN from our loft building, in Center City
Philadelphia, stands a studio building. I am in that building almost
every day because I have an art studio there. My rowing machine is
also there for my daily exercise, as well as a podcast studio. I keep the
keys that I need to get in to these studios on one key chain. A few
months ago my keys disappeared. Luella and I looked and looked,
but we never found them. This meant I couldn't exercise or paint.
I reached out to the owner of the building and two weeks later had a
new set of keys. In the scheme of things, this wasn't a very big personal
crisis, but it was frustrating. In the middle of my search, it struck me
that I have such an utter lack of sovereignty that I can't even control
my keys. It takes divine grace for me to be able to control myself, let
alone exercise any control over the people and situations in my life.
I have no idea what is coming down the road, and I have little ability
to stop most of it even if I did. But I am not anxious or hopeless.

Because I am God's child, my peace of heart doesn't rest on my control over my life. My rest is in my Savior, who rules over everything, everywhere, all of the time. I have peace because I will never be in a situation, location, or relationship that isn't under his wise rule. Perhaps the best summary of the extent of God's sovereignty over everything is found in Daniel 4.

At the end of the days I, Nebuchadnezzar, lifted my eyes to heaven, and my reason returned to me, and I blessed the Most High, and praised and honored him who lives forever,

> for his dominion is an everlasting dominion,
>   and his kingdom endures from generation to generation;
> all the inhabitants of the earth are accounted as nothing,
>   and he does according to his will among the host of
>   heaven
>   and among the inhabitants of the earth;
> and none can stay his hand
>   or say to him, "What have you done?" (Dan. 4:34–35)

It is such an encouragement to wake up in the morning and know that all the things in your life that are out of your control are not out of control. All of the things that are out of your control are under the control of one who is the definition of everything that is wise and good, right and true. God's exercise of his sovereignty is perfect in every way, because God is perfectly holy in every way. This doesn't mean that you will always understand what God brings into your life or what he ordains for his world. It may look at times that what God ordains is anything but good. God's sovereignty may be confusing, but it is never evil. Because God's secret will is secret for our good, knowing that God is sovereign does not mean that you and I will understand all the things that God ordains for us to experience. So, our rest is found not in our understanding, but in trusting in the one who understands it all and rules it all for his glory and our good.

We need to be reminded again and again that peace of heart is found not in figuring everything out in life, but in entrusting ourselves to the one who has everything figured out. This is one of the important purposes of corporate worship. I think of corporate worship as being like a conversation I used to have with my children when they were young. Sometimes I would have to say no to our children. They would ask me why I said no, but I knew they were too young to understand my explanation. So I would say to them, "Is your daddy a bad daddy?" They would say, "No, you're not a bad daddy." I would say, "Does your daddy like to do bad things to you?" They would say, "No, Daddy." I would say, "Does your daddy like to make you sad?" They would say, "No, Daddy." I would say, "Do you know your daddy loves you?" They would say, "Yes, Daddy." Then I would say, "Because I love you, I have chosen to say no to you, and I know you don't understand why. Now, you can think, 'My daddy is a bad daddy because he says no to me,' or you can think, 'I don't know why my daddy said no to me, but I know he loves me.'"

This conversation brings together three things we need that the gathering of the church reminds us of again and again. First, the one who rules our lives, often in ways we don't understand, is our Father. By grace, we are the children of the one who sits on the throne of the universe, exercising rule over everything. He is not some distant and unapproachable King. For us, because of his amazing adopting grace, his rule is Father-rule. Second, his rule is wise. Many things lie beyond our capacity to know and understand, but God understands. His sovereignty means he unleashes his wisdom to guide his world. He always ordains what is wisest and best, even if it doesn't always seem best to us. Finally, his rule never contradicts or abandons his love. The sovereign one rules his world out of love for his children, and his rule will lead his children to a final kingdom where peace and righteousness reign forever and ever.

Corporate worship should remind us that our rule is small, weak, and inadequate, and then comfort us with the grand, glorious, and eternal rule of our Father over all that has been, all that is, and all that forever will be.

———

Scripture: 1 Timothy 6:15–16 and Jude 1:25

Reflections: Do you find comfort in the words of Daniel 4:34–35? Why or why not?

Family Discussion: Talk about whether it is easy or difficult for you to entrust yourselves and those things that are out of your control to your Savior.

Sunday 43

Corporate worship is designed to enthrall you with the ever-faithful, always-patient, still-abounding love of your Lord and Savior.

A WORSHIP SERVICE was the last place I wanted to be, but I went because Luella strongly encouraged me to go. I dreaded anyone asking me how I was doing. I dreaded the long walk up the stairs. I dreaded sitting so long in one place. I was embarrassed that I was too weak to stand through the congregational singing part of the service. I didn't like feeling and looking like an infirm old man. I walked into that worship service with a complaining heart and grumbling on my lips. I was in no condition to worship.

I had recently gotten out of the hospital—again. I was physically exhausted and emotionally discouraged. I was tired of being sick all the time, but with the cycle of endless surgeries, that had been my world for what I considered way too long. I walked into that service with a drainage bag strapped to my leg, a physical reminder that I was not okay. I had so many questions and fears. I had gone from being very physically fit for my age to being chronically sick, with little relief in sight. I wasn't mad at God; I was just beaten down, and the last thing I wanted to do was participate in a worship service.

I know that many of my brothers and sisters have found themselves in the same place, either because of physical illness or because of the many other hardships of life in this fallen world. One woman told me that she dreaded going to her church service and seeing all the happy married couples; her husband had forsaken her. A depressed man told me he dreaded singing the hymns that made him face how far God seemed to be from him. Another man, who had been eighteen months without work, told me he had a hard time getting excited about singing about how God was faithful and good.

Yes, we often come to worship weary, bruised, weakened, and feeling alone. We often struggle to go, or wonder why we're there. Sometimes it seems easier to avoid God and the gathering of his people. Sometimes the truths of God's word don't encourage us as they once did. And sometimes prayer is more of a burdensome duty than a joy.

Could it be that those times are the times when we most desperately need to be in worship gatherings? Could it be, in those times of spiritual struggle, that the things we tend to dread are the very things that we need? Could it be that corporate worship is designed for the weak, the discouraged, and the weary? Could it be that this is exactly why God gifted us with his church and its regular gathering for worship? Could it be that the gathering of God's people for worship and instruction provide just the medicine we need?

Let me tell you what happened to me on that particular difficult Sunday. I began to hear, from the voices of my brothers and sisters lifted up in song, what my soul so desperately needed to

hear. I needed to hear that the love of God would not let me go.
I needed to hear that he would never leave me alone. I needed to
hear that he rules over heaven and earth. I needed to hear of his
Fatherly care. My bruised heart needed the salve of the gospel of
God's presence, power, love, and grace. I needed preaching that
confronted me with a kingdom bigger than my own, ruled by one
who is the definition of wisdom and love. I needed to hear the
gospel not in some abstract theological form, but at street level:
God for me, God with me.

As I listened, the posture of my heart began to change. Not
everything changed; I was still in the middle of something very
difficult, and I would be tempted again to despise my weakness
and lose sight of God's goodness. But I had been given a great gift.
In that worship service, I was helped to see beyond the mountain
of my physical and spiritual difficulties and to see my Savior and
the right-here, right-now glories of his grace. I know I will need
to get gospel perspective again and again, and I'm sure you share
that need. I will always need to be reminded that, no matter what
I am facing, I am eternally loved by God. And that reality changes
the experience of everything in my life.

When I think back on that once-dreaded Sunday, Psalm 42
comes to my mind. Read and reread it, and then run to the assembly
of God's people. Drag yourself there if you have to, but go. That
assembly is a gift of God's grace to his weary children.

> As a deer pants for flowing streams,
>> so pants my soul for you, O God.
> My soul thirsts for God,
>> for the living God.
> When shall I come and appear before God?

My tears have been my food
   day and night,
while they say to me all the day long,
   "Where is your God?"
These things I remember,
   as I pour out my soul:
how I would go with the throng
   and lead them in procession to the house of God
with glad shouts and songs of praise,
   a multitude keeping festival.

Why are you cast down, O my soul,
   and why are you in turmoil within me?
Hope in God; for I shall again praise him,
   my salvation and my God.

My soul is cast down within me;
   therefore I remember you
from the land of Jordan and of Hermon,
   from Mount Mizar.
Deep calls to deep
   at the roar of your waterfalls;
all your breakers and your waves
   have gone over me.
By day the LORD commands his steadfast love,
   and at night his song is with me,
   a prayer to the God of my life.
I say to God, my rock:
   "Why have you forgotten me?

Why do I go mourning
    because of the oppression of the enemy?"
As with a deadly wound in my bones,
    my adversaries taunt me,
while they say to me all the day long,
    "Where is your God?"

Why are you cast down, O my soul,
    and why are you in turmoil within me?
Hope in God; for I shall again praise him,
    my salvation and my God. (Ps. 42)

———

Scripture: Psalm 73:21–28

Reflections: How has gathering with God's people been a help to you during a difficult time in your life?

Family Discussion: Which verses in Psalm 42 or Psalm 73 do you most resonate with and why?

Sunday 44

Corporate worship is designed to create a rest of heart in you, not because you've become able, but because your Lord is able, ready, and willing, and he has poured down his glory on you for your eternal good.

I WEAR A FITNESS RING. It is an amazing piece of modern technology. One of the things my ring does is chart my sleep. It tells me how well I rested, that is, how much of my sleep has been deep, light, or REM sleep. My ring has alerted me to how important physical rest is. It has reminded me how much the body needs a regular time to rejuvenate and recharge. You and I cannot live well without sleep and the physical rest that is so essential to our physical health and well-being. On evenings when I am very tired and fall exhausted into my bed, I often tell Luella how thankful I am for a bed and how grateful I am that God created sleep. Physical rest is a needful and beautiful thing.

But physical rest is not all that we need to function properly. Spiritual rest, that is, rest of heart and mind is even more important. We don't live well, we don't relate to others well, we don't make decisions well, and we don't commune with God well when our hearts are not at rest. Often it is the cares and burdens of life that rob us of rest of heart. Perhaps an ongoing marriage struggle robs you of your joy and produces a debilitating combination of fear and anger. Maybe it is the seemingly unceasing burdens of parenting, that endless catalog of "what-ifs" that create parental anxiety. Or maybe you're just tired of loading the burden of your children's welfare on your shoulders every morning. It could be the daily stresses of your job. You heart tenses up as you drive into the parking lot, knowing what you're going to face yet another day. Perhaps physical sickness has introduced you to a world of worry. Maybe you pay too much attention to the state of the world around you and carry the burden of things over which you have no control. Maybe you wake up anxious because you know you don't have money to cover the bills, and you are already dreading the phone calls that are sure to come. You may have been betrayed by a friend, and your sad heart plays the scene of that betrayal over and over again. Maybe you've experienced more anxiety at your university than you ever thought you would experience, and you're emotionally worn down. It could be the weaknesses of old age have robbed you of your joy.

Life in this broken, dysfunctional world is not easy. We all face things that confound and confuse us. We all face things for which we feel unprepared. We all carry concerns that are bigger than our ability to solve. We all are confronted by our weaknesses. We all cry out for wisdom and wish we had more strength. We all wish we could change things that we have no ability to alter. We all wonder if we have taken on too much. We all face situations we wish we could get ourselves out of. We all experience moments when we feel small and unable. We all have seasons of worry, where the burdens of life right here, right now are getting the best of us. None of us always feel wise, strong, and capable. None of us.

You may be thinking, "Then how is rest of heart possible?" I am convinced that beneath much of my fear, worry, and concern is self-reliance. Much of what causes my heart to lack rest is my assessment of inability.

I don't like being confused.
I don't like feeling as if I lack wisdom.
I don't like being weak.
I don't like thinking things are out of my control.
I don't like feeling unprepared.
I don't like being afraid.
I don't like feeing unable.

I want to be independently strong, wise, and able, and when I'm not, it is hard for my heart to be at rest. It is at the epicenter of this spiritual struggle that the gospel of God's presence and grace meets me. The gospel teaches me that the deepest rest of heart is not found in independent strength and ability. No, true, unshakable rest of heart is found in remembering and celebrating that God is able and that he is with me, in me, and for me. I have hope not because I am independently capable, but because he has invaded my life with his presence, his power, his promises, and his grace. He does in me, for me, and through me what I could never do in and of myself. He is strong when I am weak. He understands what confuses me. He is active when I am too exhausted to do anything. He is wise when I am foolish. He wins victories when I feel defeated. Nothing can stop his redeeming plan, nothing can thwart his holy will. In grace he unleashes his glory on me. He is my protection, he is my strength, he is my wisdom, he is my guide, and he is my rest.

When I shift my confidence in him to myself, my rest of heart fades away. But when I remember him and trust in him, even though there is much I don't understand and many places where I feel unable, my heart can still rest. Why? Because God exists, and he is my Father.

Last Sunday, in our church's worship service, we sang a song about the rest that is found in remembering that God is sovereign, that he rules everything, and that he rules it all for the good of the children of his love. As we sang, I knew I needed to be in that gathering, if for no other reason than to remember my Lord's reign and to wrap the blanket of that truth around my heart and rest. I'm sure you need that reminder—and the rest too.

———

Scripture: Matthew 11:28–30

Reflections: In what areas of life are you relying on your own strength and ability rather than trusting in God?

Family Discussion: Share a situation in which your heart was able to rest after you remembered that God is with you, in you, and for you.

Sunday 45

Corporate worship is designed to remind you to
stop taking credit for what you could have never
produced on your own and to bow before your Savior
of faithful, patient, powerful, and generous grace.

IT HAS HAPPENED to all of us: someone takes credit for something we have done. You find it hard to believe. You want to yell at the person: "What are you doing? I'm the one that got it done." But you don't say anything. You sit in your hurt, trying your best to hide the emotions that are welling up inside of you. In a fallen world populated by flawed people, it's hard to avoid these moments. We learn from the garden of Eden that the source of all sin is pride. Adam and Eve wanted God's position. They were not content with their life of dependency, so they stepped over God's boundaries and consumed what was forbidden. Pride deceives you into thinking that you deserve what you don't deserve and that you're capable of doing what you could never do on your own. All of us have times when we rewrite our histories to make ourselves more of the hero than we actually were. We minimize the actions and contributions of others while dramatizing the importance of ours. Sin makes us love being on center stage with the spotlight on us.

In this way humility is a spiritual battleground. Sin makes humility unnatural for us. Sin makes us think we are better and more capable than we actually are. Sin makes fools think they are wise. Sin convinces the weak that they are strong. Sin causes us to think that we are way more righteous than we actually are. Sin causes us to minimize our sin, while we quickly point out the sin of others. Sin makes us think we are entitled to things we haven't earned and don't deserve. Sin causes us to hate to admit we are unable. Sin makes us defensive when corrected. Sin pushes us away from humility and confession of need and toward self-righteousness and self-sufficiency. Sin makes us quick to take credit, but slow to admit blame. Pride is a liar, so it is sin's propellant. Pride never produces a harvest of good fruit.

The problem for most of us is that the pride of taking credit for what we could never do on our own most often doesn't live in the big, dramatic moments of our lives. No, it lives in the small wrinkles of the fabric of every day. If you have a good, peaceful marriage, you can't take credit for it, because you have no ability to control the heart, mind, and choices of your spouse. It's easy to take pride in the fact that your children are doing well, but the truth is that no matter how well you act toward your children, if they don't transact with God then they won't do well; and you can't make that transaction for them. If your job or career is going well, you must humbly admit there are so many economic, industrial, governmental, and commercial forces over which you have no control that contribute to your success. If you have experienced success in ministry, then praise goes to your Lord, for he alone controls when the winds of the Spirit will blow, causing people to respond. If you have experienced good health, it is important to remember that every fiber of your body lives under the rule of the Creator. This list could go on and on.

Now, in each of these areas you *are* making important contributions. Your thoughts, desires, choices, actions, and words are important, but none of these are enough of an explanation for the good things you have experienced. The worldview of the Bible, the way that God describes how the world he created functions, doesn't allow us to stand in the middle of our lives and say, "Look at the wonderful things that I have independently created." In fact, independence is a delusion. Even Adam and Eve, who were perfect people living in a perfect world, were dependent on God. And when, for a moment, they thought that they were smarter than God and opted for independent living, disaster was the result.

In every area of your life you can see things that are beyond your control, things that must work well in order for your life to be livable and for you to have peace of any kind. The book of Romans includes a doxology that speaks powerfully to this issue of where the good things in our lives originate: "For from him and through him and to him are all things. To him be glory forever. Amen" (Rom. 11:36).

Corporate worship is designed to remind us that everything we use and depend on every day has come from the hand of the Lord. He is not only the wise and powerful Creator, but he is also the loving and generous provider. He provides what we need to do what he calls us to do, even on days when we forget him. Without his creation and his continual provision, we would have nothing. It is also true that everything comes through him. Yes, every good and perfect gift comes from above (James 1:17). Our Lord doesn't just provide; he works in and through what he has provided, doing for us what we cannot do for ourselves. His hand is in everything we do, in everything we create, and in every good result. But there is one more thing that corporate worship reminds us of. If everything comes from his hand and everything depends on his activity in our behalf, then the glory, honor, and praise goes to him and not to us. Here's why this is so important. The pride of taking credit crushes a life a joyful trust and willing dependency on the Lord. We therefore gather so we would feel rightfully small, our Lord would loom appropriately large, and our faith in him would grow increasingly stronger. As we walk away from another service of worship and instruction, may the words of Romans 11:36 be in our hearts and on our lips: for from you and through you and to you are all things. To you be the glory forever. Amen.

———

Scripture: Romans 12:3 and Philippians 2:3–4

Reflections: What does taking credit for something do to our faith in God? Why is this significant?

Family Discussion: Talk about the difference between making important contributions and taking credit for independently creating or accomplishing something.

Sunday 46

Corporate worship is designed to make the knowledge of
God the most life-shaping body of knowledge in your life.

MY MOM AND DAD named me Paul David. These were not random
names that simply sounded nice to them, nor were they family
names. They chose these names because they marked out something
very significant in my parents' lives. Right before I was born, Mom
and Dad had made a profession of faith, so they wanted to choose
names for me that depicted their newfound faith. They opted for
not just biblical names, but two of the most prominent names
in all of Scripture. David, writer of great psalms, musician, poet,
and shepherd, received the promise that his kingdom would never
end. Jesus, Son of David, was born in David's line. There would
be no redemptive story, no Messiah, no cross, and no empty tomb
without David. I carry a regal and a deeply spiritual name, David,
the man after God's own heart.

Then there is my first name, Paul. The apostle Paul wrote more
New Testament books than any other writer. God chose Paul to
expound and explain the mysteries of the gospel, the essentiality

and structure of the church, and what it looks like to live in light of the gospel in your daily life. We learn about marriage, parenting, being a citizen, working as unto the Lord, our world of talk, spiritual warfare, and much more from Paul. I have spent my adult life and ministry sitting at the feet of the apostle whose name I bear, deeply grateful for what I have learned that I would not know if God hadn't chosen, gifted, and inspired him to write all of those epistles. I am grateful for the young faith of my parents that birthed in them the desire to give me names that mean something.

Though I love the meaning of my names, I realize the names of God are far more meaningful and significant. Through his names, God reveals to us what he is, who he is, and what he does. Here's why this is so important. One of the primary goals of the church and its regular gatherings is to instill and deepen in us a knowledge of God. No body of knowledge is more essential to human thinking, understanding, and living than the knowledge of God. God is the ultimate fact that gives meaning and understanding to every other fact that your mind could consider. There is no real human knowing that doesn't begin with knowing God. Omitting God from the way you understand the world is like an accountant ignoring a number in a column of figures he is calculating. No matter how accurately he has added the numbers in the column, his total at the bottom will always be wrong, because he has omitted an essential fact. So, we can't understand our identity, meaning, and purpose; we can't understand relationships and family; we can't understand sexuality and money; we can't understand religion, politics, or government without starting with the existence, character, and plan of the one who created it all. We won't properly understand our spirituality, emotionality, physicality, personality, rationality, or psychology without starting with the Creator of all of these things. Without the boundaries set by the knowledge of God, human rationality will always lead to irrationality.

Because knowing God is so essential to everything we are and everything we are meant to do, God has designed his church, through worship and instruction, guided by his word, to continually be growing our knowledge of him. One of the ways the church does this is by singing and expounding of the names of God. Consider the following:[1]

- Elohim: The Mighty One (Gen. 1:1)
- El-Shaddai: God Almighty (Gen. 17:1)
- Jehovah Jireh: The Lord Our Provider (Gen. 22:14)
- Jehovah Rapha: The Lord Our Healer (Ex. 15:26)
- Jehovah Nissi: The Lord Our Banner (Ex. 17:15)
- Jehovah Shalom: The Lord Our Peace (Judges 6:24)
- Adonai: Lord (1 Sam. 24:8)
- Jehovah Raah: The Lord Our Shepherd (Ps. 23:1)
- El Elyon: God Most High (Ps. 57:2)
- Immanuel: God with Us (Isa. 7:14)
- Wonderful Counselor. Mighty God. Everlasting Father. Prince of Peace (Isa. 9:6)
- Jehovah Tsidkenu: The Lord Our Righteousness (Jer. 23:6)
- Jehovah Shammah: The Lord Is Here (Ezek. 48:35)
- Ancient of Days (Dan. 7)
- Jesus: He Shall Save His People from Their Sins (Matt. 1:21)
- The Good Shepherd (John 10:11)

---

1 The following list was compiled with help from Danielle Bernock's "What Are the Names of God Found in the Bible?," *Christianity.com*, September 9, 2022, www.christianity.com.

- Abba Father (Rom. 8:15)
- Lion of Judah (Rev. 5:5)
- Alpha and Omega: The First and the Last, the Beginning and the End (Rev. 22:13)

There is so much to be known about God just from the names by which he has chosen to identify himself. He is our provider, healer, shepherd, and peace. He is the Lord, the Almighty, the Savior who is with us. He is our Father, our counselor, and our King. Everything that we need, we find in him. Nothing is more important than knowing God. So we gather to learn of him and to sing his names into one another's ears. We gather to celebrate that he, in his shining glory, is *for us*, his children—because of his amazing grace. As we grow to know him, we also grow in understanding the wonder of what it means to be known *by* him. God included the legacy of his names in his Word because he wants us to know him and he wants us to meditate together on how wonderful it is that the one depicted by these names is, by grace, our Father.

———

Scripture: John 17:3 and 2 Peter 1:2–8

Reflections: Which of the listed names of God is unfamiliar to you? Try reading the corresponding passage to gain further insight.

Family Discussion: Discuss the importance of starting with God when trying to explain or understand ourselves, others, and the world around us.

Sunday 47

Corporate worship is designed to hold before
you the unstoppable grace that is your hope
for today and all the days to come.

MY WIFE AND I LIKE TO buy flowers from the market because we like the beauty of fresh flowers in our loft. But buying fresh flowers is a lesson in decay. After a few days our floral arrangements need some editing to discard the wilted blossoms. Then my wife puts what is left of the bouquet in a much smaller vase. Finally, with all the flowers now dead, we debate whether we should display the remaining greenery that is still fresh. So it is with many of the beautiful things in our lives, including us. Luella and I have been gathering early marriage pictures, and the evidence is quite clear: sadly, we too, are in the process of decay. Someday our physical bodies will give way, and we will cross over to the other side.

Your sweater becomes stretched and frayed, and you don't wear it anymore. The food you took home from the restaurant languishes in the refrigerator until you notice that it is spoiled and you throw it away. Your new car doesn't look or smell new for very long, and eventually enough parts malfunction that you conclude it's not worth repairing anymore. Friendships come and go, never staying with us as long as we wished. We all spend time in moments of nostalgia, looking back at what once was, but is no more.

This side of eternity we all live with impermanence. We all have to learn to accept the temporary. We learn that what was once trustworthy doesn't always remain trustworthy. Things that we depend on cease to deliver. Our dresser drawers, pantries, and garages are archaeological museums of artifacts of a civilization that once was. Old cell phones, old glasses, old clothes, old dishes, old appliances, old exercise equipment, and all kinds of old and outdated technology litter our homes. No longer usable, no longer dependable, and no longer needed, we stuff them someplace and move on. We've grown accustomed to the fact that things don't last, things stop working.

It's harder when the thing that doesn't last is a treasured friendship or family bond. You can't stuff a friend who has moved on into your garage and walk away. We all carry the sadness and scars of the precious ones that time, distance, change, and sin have robbed us of. Some of us are so scarred that we are afraid to be vulnerable, we're afraid to open our hearts again, and we're afraid to commit to anyone. I remember sitting with a shocked and bitter husband, whose wife had left after twenty-two years. He said, "I've been taken once, and it will never happen to me again." I understood how deeply hurt he was, but I was also aware of how alone he was committing himself to be. Human love had failed him, so he had exited himself from human love to avoid being hurt again. Many of us are carrying around family, friendship, or church hurt. Many of us, because of our hurts, have become more private, more self-protective, and less willing to open our hearts. Many of us carry relational scars into new relationships, not willing to be vulnerable like we once were. Many of us have decided that being alone is safer than being together. Many of us don't know how to repair what was broken or how to restore what is now shattered. Many of us don't know how to move forward. Many of us wonder whom we can trust.

For many of us, the hurt we have experienced in human relationships has impacted our relationship with God. We struggle to give ourselves fully to our Lord, because we wonder if he will leave us too. When God calls himself our Father, we immediately remember the failures of our earthly father, and we wonder. When Jesus tells us that he is our friend, we remember our history of failed friendships, and we wonder. When God calls us to hold on to his promises, we remember so many unfulfilled promises of so many people, and we wonder. We have been hurt, so we stand on the spiritual sidelines, afraid of entrusting ourselves fully to our heavenly Father.

So we need to gather with other hurt ones who, like us, have experienced the devastating disappointments of life in this fallen world. We remember together that God is not like our friends or family. He is perfectly faithful in every way and all of the time. He keeps every single one of his promises, and he will never forsake his children. We need, in song and word, to be reminded of the truths of God's unstoppable grace and inseparable love again and again. These truths are beautifully captured for us in Romans 8:28–39:

And we know that for those who love God all things work together for good, for those who are called according to his purpose. For those whom he foreknew he also predestined to be conformed to the image of his Son, in order that he might be the firstborn among many brothers. And those whom he predestined he also called, and those whom he called he also justified, and those whom he justified he also glorified.

What then shall we say to these things? If God is for us, who can be against us? He who did not spare his own Son but gave him up for us all, how will he not also with him graciously give us all things? Who shall bring any charge against God's elect? It is God who justifies. Who is to condemn? Christ Jesus is the one who died—more than that, who was raised—who is at the right hand of God, who indeed is interceding for us. Who shall separate us from the love of Christ? Shall tribulation, or distress, or persecution, or famine, or nakedness, or danger, or sword? As it is written,

> "For your sake we are being killed all the day long;
>   we are regarded as sheep to be slaughtered."

No, in all these things we are more than conquerors through him who loved us. For I am sure that neither death nor life, nor angels nor rulers, nor things present nor things to come, nor powers, nor height nor depth, nor anything else in all creation, will be able to separate us from the love of God in Christ Jesus our Lord.

May we gather and remember that the love of our heavenly Father is not like human love. May we gather and remember that nothing can ever stop the march of his grace and nothing can separate us from his love. May we gather and remember that God loves us so much that not only did he give us his Son—not only will he freely provide for us everything we need—but he will also work in all things for our eternal good. May we gather again and again, marinating in the truth of his perfect love, so that our hurt can be transformed by the gospel into bright and unshakable hope.

———

Scripture: Lamentations 3:21–24, Romans 15:13, and Hebrews 10:23–25

Reflections: What past relational hurts are preventing you from giving yourself fully to the Lord? How can gathering with God's people help to remedy that?

Family Discussion: Discuss ways we can be reminded of God's perfect love, grace, and provision.

Sunday 48

Corporate worship is designed to move you from a life of independence to a life of humble, willing, joyful, and consistent dependence on God.

If a plant is to fruit and flower,
it needs water
to feed and nourish its roots.
Waterless, it will wither and die
before it buds.
Every muscle of the body,
to do its work,
needs strength and growth-giving nutrients.
Void of nutrition, it will weaken and atrophy,
unable to withstand its assigned work.
Every part of the body
cannot properly function
without every other part of the body,
never doing its work in isolation,
always in connection and cooperation.

Every soft and malleable lump of clay
needs the skilled hands of a potter.
Clay has no capacity
to form itself into something
useful and beautiful.
Sheep weren't created
to shepherd themselves.
They were made to be
cared for,
fed,
guided,
protected.
No infant comes into the world
self-parenting.
Each is born with a desperate need
for the constant nurturing care
of a loving parent's hand.
Look around at God's wide and varied creation,
examine each thing, and you will discover need.
According to the Creator's design,
nothing exists on its own.
There is no such thing as
independence.
Everything God created is dependent
in some way.
That sad moment in the garden
stands as a forever reminder
that independence is dangerous,
attractive,
seductive,

deceptive,
destructive,
delusion,
which will always lead you away from
your Creator,
your created purpose:
mutually dependent community.
So today remind yourself again,
you're the plant in constant need
of living water.
Your muscles are weak apart from the nutrients of grace.
You're a part of a body,
needing every other part
to do your part.
You're clay in need
of the Potter's skilled hands.
You're a sheep in need of
the Shepherd's care.
You're the child in need of
the Father's nurture.
Willing,
humble,
joyful,
infant-like
dependence
opens the door
to your Father's care
and to all of the provisions of grace
he has made,
he is making,

and he will continue to make
for each one of his children.
Remind yourself
that you weren't designed
to make it on your own.
You were made needy so that
neediness would drive you to your Creator,
to find all that you ever need in him.
Consider again the dependence of everything
and be warned.
The delusion of independence
will never ever take you anywhere good.

May we joyfully gather and remember that God daily protects us as we grapple with the seductive delusion of independence and celebrate together the grace that has wooed us again and again into the rest and security of dependence on God.

———

Scripture: Proverbs 3:5–6

Reflections: How have you seen your humble dependence upon God open the door to his care, provision, and grace?

Family Discussion: List several things in creation and talk about what they depend upon for survival. Whom do you depend upon? Why were we made needy?

Sunday 49

Corporate worship is designed to stimulate you to make
sure your life today is shaped by the surety and glory of
what God has promised you on that final tomorrow.

After this I looked, and behold, a great multitude that no one
could number, from every nation, from all tribes and peoples
and languages, standing before the throne and before the Lamb,
clothed in white robes, with palm branches in their hands, and
crying out with a loud voice, "Salvation belongs to our God who
sits on the throne, and to the Lamb!" And all the angels were
standing around the throne and around the elders and the four
living creatures, and they fell on their faces before the throne and
worshiped God, saying, "Amen! Blessing and glory and wisdom
and thanksgiving and honor and power and might be to our God
forever and ever! Amen." (Rev. 7:9–12)

We are invited, by means of God's word, to look into this
amazing celestial scene. The redeemed of the Lord have gathered
before God's throne. They represent every period of history,

every place on the globe, every ethnicity, and every language. The blood of the Lamb paid for their right to be there. They are overwhelmed with gratitude and cannot do anything but worship. The only thing that comes out of their mouths are words of praise—no complaints in this moment, no "what-ifs" or "if onlys." They are experiencing the final satisfaction of redemption. They are the benefactors of the ultimate victory. This is the celebration of celebrations, the party of parties. This is the ultimate worship service, the final gathering of God's children, and this one will last forever. Salvation is complete. God has won!

No matter where we find ourselves in the Bible, we should always ask why God chose the particular things that we're reading to be recorded for us. We are invited into this particular scene—the celebration of the completion of God's work of redemption—so that we would know that the present moment we're in is not all that there is. It is vital to know that God is still at work, completing what he has begun, and that he will not stop until sin and Satan are finally and forever defeated. The reason it is essential to know this is so that we would live right here, right now with eternity in view. This frees us from living with a destination focus rather than a preparation focus. Living with a destination focus means you pour all of your hope and dreams into this present moment, spending all of your time and energy on your personal definition of pleasure, comfort, and success. This means you live to acquire, possess, and experience, with no grander agenda than your own happiness. If this is all there is, then it makes sense to live for the happiness and pleasure of this moment.

Sadly, many of us get sucked into a functional eternity agnosticism. It's not that we don't theologically believe in eternity; the "not yet" might be an important piece of our formal spiritual confession. But when it comes to the way we live, the things we want, the circumstances that scare us, the things that make us happy, and the situations that disappoint, we live as if eternity doesn't exist. We allow the culture around us, which has long since denied the existence of any meaningful afterlife, to define for us what the good life is. We allow influencers to tell us that we need this or that in order to be truly fulfilled. So, although we say we believe in eternity, where the rubber meets the road in our daily choices and actions, we act as if eternity doesn't exist.

Living with a preparation focus means we know that this is not all there is. God's work in us and in his world is not complete. He is still on the throne, he is still putting enemies under his feet, and he will reign until the last enemy has been defeated. Then he will bring all things to a final end and welcome us into his forever kingdom. This means that this moment is not about how much I can acquire and experience, but rather about God working, by grace, to make me ready for what is to come. I am not yet fit for the glory that is coming for me, so God will take me places I didn't want to go in order to further prepare me for what is to come. So, in the locations and relationships I interact with every day, growth in God's grace becomes way more important to me than the temporary happiness I might get from here-and-now people, places, or things. My highest joy is not found in what I possess or achieve, but in his presence, his love, his forgiving and transforming grace, his truth, and his unstoppable, redemptive plan. Living with a preparation focus means that the final scenes of redemptive celebration in Revelation 7 influence my values in situations, locations, and relationships right now.

This is a struggle for me. The things of this earth tug at me. The enjoyment of the moment can mean too much to me. The pursuit of the next pleasure can control too much of me. The next personal achievement can become too important to me. Now, it's not wrong to enjoy things on this earth, but once they control you, you forget who you are, you forget what God is doing, and you forget where you're heading. I'm sure there are ways in which we are never completely free of functional eternity agnosticism.

So God has blessed us with his church and its constant gatherings for worship, instruction, and fellowship. He's given us his church to keep the surety and glory of eternity ever before us. He's given his church so that, together with brothers and sisters in Christ, we now join the voices that are to come and sing songs of redemptive celebration. He's given us his church so that our pastors and preachers point us again and again to what is to come and warn us again and again of the dangers of living only for the present. He's given us his church so that we would live with the security of knowing that God will not relent until every cell of the hearts of all of his children are forever sin free. He's given us his church, and for we who often forget the eternity that is to come, that is a very good thing.

———

Scripture: John 12:25 and 2 Corinthians 4:17–18

Reflections: How does the church help us to live with eternity in view? How can you encourage others to live this way?

Family Discussion: Talk about what functional eternity agnosticism is and why it is so easy to get sucked into it.

Sunday 50

Corporate worship is designed to help you evaluate
the difficulties and disappointments of the present
in light of the incalculable glory that is to come.

JOEY WALKED OUT of his boss's office without a job. His shock
kept him from absorbing exactly what this meant. He loved his
work, and he was good at it. Over the years he had collected many
accolades and several promotions. He thought he was set, that this
would be his life work. Joey had not anticipated or prepared for this
moment. His boss was kind, but that didn't cushion the blow. Their
industry had radically changed over the last ten years, and Joey's
firm decided to close an entire division. Those industry changes
and his firm's decision meant that Joey not only lost a job, but it
would be hard for him to find a new job in his field of expertise.
As he packed up his office, anger bubbled up inside of him. Why?
What had his hard work gotten him?

Rose was committed to regular exercise. On Saturday that meant getting on her road bike and doing a ten-mile sprint. One beautiful spring morning the wind whistled in her ears and the spring buds were a blur as she flew by. She was thinking that it probably didn't get any better than this, when she heard a screeching sound and then everything went black. A distracted driver had slammed into her, changing her life forever. She awoke in the hospital, disoriented and afraid. After she had been awake for a few hours, plagued by a thousand questions, her surgeon came and told her that it was a miracle she had survived such a violent hit, but that he had bad news. They were unable to save her left leg; it had been amputated above the knee. She was beyond crushed. When the doctor left, the tears came, and they continued to flow for several hours. "Why?" she cried. "Of all the people who were riding on the road, why me? What will my life look like now? Why?"

———

Jared and Sydney had tried and tried and were weary of trying. They had to accept what they couldn't control or change: they weren't going to be able to have a child of their own. All of the best medical research and intervention hadn't helped them. He tried his best to help her through this devastating disappointment, but she was inconsolable. In fact, she was angry that he didn't seem to be as crushed as she was. Her disappointment began to devolve into envy. She seethed inside every time she was near a couple with an infant or toddler. She was mad at God. "Why would he let this happen to me?"

———

Every one of us will face moments like these. Somehow, someway, suffering interrupts everyone's lives. We will all face the unexpected and unwanted. There are disappointments on the road ahead for all of us. No matter how carefully you plan your life, no matter how wise you are, and no matter what protections you put in place, you will not avoid pain. If you're not suffering now, you are near someone who is and, if you're not suffering now, it's inevitable that you will. Because this is true, it is important to understand that your life is not shaped just by what you suffer, but by how you suffer what you suffer. What you do with your suffering will have a huge impact on what your life will look like after.

We are all moral mathematicians. We constantly make value calculations. We weigh what we experience on the scales of what we think we deserve. We weigh the past from the perspective of the future. We weigh what we have been given by what God has promised. We weigh what we have to deal with by what we think we are capable of. We weigh what we should think, feel, and do with what we want or feel like doing. We evaluate our responses against the responses of others. We constantly make moral calculations that shape what we think about ourselves, our lives, our relationships, and our God.

When it comes to weighing the disappointments of life, Romans 8:18–25 is a game changer:

> For I consider that the sufferings of this present time are not worth comparing with the glory that is to be revealed to us. For the creation waits with eager longing for the revealing of the sons of God. For the creation was subjected to futility, not willingly, but because of him who subjected it, in hope that the creation itself will be set free from its bondage to corruption and

obtain the freedom of the glory of the children of God. For we know that the whole creation has been groaning together in the pains of childbirth until now. And not only the creation, but we ourselves, who have the firstfruits of the Spirit, groan inwardly as we wait eagerly for adoption as sons, the redemption of our bodies. For in this hope we were saved. Now hope that is seen is not hope. For who hopes for what he sees? But if we hope for what we do not see, we wait for it with patience.

Notice what Paul does first in this passage. He assumes the universality of suffering. He doesn't start with, "For the few of you who may be suffering." He assumes that all of his readers are experientially acquainted with what he is writing about. He knows they will experience suffering because they live in a broken, groaning world and, because they do, they too will groan.

But, importantly, Paul knows that his readers will work to make sense of their suffering, that they will do value calculations. So he reminds them that these hard moments can't stand up in comparison to the endless, suffering-free years that are their destiny because they are the children of God. If there is no eternity, if this moment is all I have, then the burden of suffering is all the greater. But if this hard moment is but a blip in comparison to the eternal existence that is mine by grace, then I experience my sufferings in a very different way.

So we gather again and again to be reminded that our hardships aren't ultimate; God is. Our difficulties won't last forever but we will, eons beyond these dark days. We gather with other sufferers to be reminded once again that we will never understand our sufferings properly, evaluate them appropriately, or experience them hopefully until we look at them through the lens of the glorious destiny that is our guaranteed destination because of the gift of the grace of Jesus. We will someday join that eternal gathering, surrounded by incalculable glories, singing songs of redemption. The tears of our suffering, now dried, will be but a flash of a moment in our very distant past. We gather to remember what is to come, so we don't lose hope as we deal with the hardships that are ours now.

Scripture: Philippians 3:8–11

Reflections: How does Romans 8:18–25 adjust how you weigh or make sense of your suffering?

Family Discussion: After reading Philippians 3:8–11, talk about how the apostle Paul was able to experience hope in his suffering.

Sunday 51

*Corporate worship is designed to remind us
again and again that we rest in, worship,
and serve a risen, reigning Savior.*

WE ALL HAVE TRANSFORMATIONAL moments in our lives that
we can look back on. One of mine is the moment at summer
camp when I saw my sin and for the first time cried out for God's
forgiveness. Others include a call to ministry I sensed throughout
college, the day I married my lifelong partner and best friend, the
afternoon a tenderhearted man spoke words of encouragement to
me, a discouraged pastor, that prevented me from running away
from ministry, and the moment I received a life-altering physical
diagnosis. These were significant moments in my life that I have
never forgotten. Each of these contributed to who I am, what my
life is like, and what I do. For me they are dramatically important—but they aren't to anyone else. My big moments have no

cultural, historical, or cosmic significance whatsoever. They are just my personal milestones.

But there is one person's moment that is the most important and essential moment in human history. You could argue that the hope of every human being who ever lived depends on this moment. Without this moment, there would be no help for fallen humanity and no promise that the cosmos, severely damaged by sin, will be finally and completely renewed. Without this moment, Christian theology is a rather worthless exercise in religious gymnastics. Without this moment, the Bible is worth little more than the value of the paper it's written on. Without this moment, the faith you've put in God is in vain. Without this moment, you and I are spiritually dead and still trapped in sin's prison. Without this moment, Christianity sits on a shelf with the myriad of other hopes and dreams that have come and gone. Without this moment, we really are without God and without hope in the world.

One of the most significant and essential contributions of regular corporate worship is to put before us over and over again that we gather to worship and learn from a risen, victorious, and reigning Savior and to help us understand the implications of his moment of ultimate victory for everything in our lives. Christian theology is resurrection theology. Christian living is resurrection living. Christian hope is resurrection hope. Gospel preaching is resurrection preaching. The strength of a Christian is resurrection power. Unless the theology of the resurrection of Jesus Christ is rooted in actual events in history, there is no reason for us to gather.

The apostle Paul describes the unparalleled significance of Christ's resurrection this way:

Now if Christ is proclaimed as raised from the dead, how can some of you say that there is no resurrection of the dead? But if there is no resurrection of the dead, then not even Christ has been raised. And if Christ has not been raised, then our preaching is in vain and your faith is in vain. We are even found to be misrepresenting God, because we testified about God that he raised Christ, whom he did not raise if it is true that the dead are not raised. For if the dead are not raised, not even Christ has been raised. And if Christ has not been raised, your faith is futile and you are still in your sins. Then those also who have fallen asleep in Christ have perished. If in Christ we have hope in this life only, we are of all people most to be pitied.

But in fact Christ has been raised from the dead, the firstfruits of those who have fallen asleep. For as by a man came death, by a man has come also the resurrection of the dead. For as in Adam all die, so also in Christ shall all be made alive. But each in his own order: Christ the firstfruits, then at his coming those who belong to Christ. Then comes the end, when he delivers the kingdom to God the Father after destroying every rule and every authority and power. For he must reign until he has put all his enemies under his feet. The last enemy to be destroyed is death. (1 Cor. 15:12–26)

I can't imagine that Paul's characterization of this moment could be any stronger. Paul says that if Christ has not been raised:

Our preaching is in vain.
Your faith is in vain.
We are found to be misrepresenting God.
You are still in your sins.

Those who have fallen asleep in Christ have perished.

If in Christ we have hope in this life only, we are of all people most to be pitied.

These are strong words to help us understand the essentiality of Christ's resurrection victory. Not only would all of the things Paul lists be true, but there would be no reigning Christ right now destroying every enemy against his rule, his people, and his kingdom. There would be no final victory and no final kingdom of righteousness and peace forever and ever. We would have no realistic hope in the present and no bright hope for the future. Moral hopelessness would be the condition of every human being between birth and death, with no hope whatsoever for the afterlife.

But Christ was raised, and that changes everything.

Everything we believe, every promise of God, every present and future hope of every believer looks to that open tomb of victory. Without it, there is no Christianity, there is no trustworthy biblical worldview, there is no hope of sin's defeat, there is no gospel, there is no church. Without the resurrection, it's all gone, a vapor of hope ending with the Messiah, locked behind stone, dead and defeated, with every promise of God dying with him. Stand outside the still-sealed tomb and then walk away: there's no life to be found there. But he was raised, the stone was rolled away, he did appear, living and speaking to many, and he did ascend to the right hand of his Father to reign in victory. We will never grow out of the need to be reminded that in a moment of history, sin and death were defeated. We gather to remember that we don't hope in a dead philosophy. Christianity is a religion of the living, with a risen, victorious, reigning Christ at the center, who now lives inside of his people, empowering them with the same power by which he was raised from the dead. Now, what would ever keep us away from celebrating this good news again and again?

———

Scripture: 1 Corinthians 15:1–5

Reflections: In what ways do you sometimes take the importance of the resurrection for granted?

Family Discussion: Discuss some of the implications of the resurrection and why it is important to remember and celebrate.

Sunday 52

CHRISTMAS

Corporate worship is designed to help you continually
focus on the one born in Bethlehem, who is the
only one who can offer you eternal forgiveness,
everlasting life, and hope that will never fade.

WHEN I WAS GROWING UP in Toledo, Ohio, my family didn't
have a lot of money. We didn't have lavish birthdays, and we
didn't take exotic vacations. We lived in an average city home on
an average block in an average neighborhood. But my mom and
dad loved Christmas. My dad loved decorating the house, and
my mom loved to make Christmas goodies. My mother and my
grandmother would get together for two weeks to do nothing but
make Christmas cookies. We loved these pre-Christmas weeks,
with the sights, sounds, and smells of the edible glories that were
to come. We were so excited when they would offer us a broken or
misshapen cookie and we tried, mostly without success, to purloin

a few when they weren't looking. When the cookies were done, Mom would hide containers all over the house so we wouldn't eat them all before the big day actually arrived. We loved the day when grandma arrived to start the baking, because we knew that Christmas wasn't far away.

Those cookies were my mom's gift to the family, but there was one particular gift on one Christmas Day that was so surprising and exciting that I have never forgotten it. I was about nine years old, and all I dreamed about was having my own brand-new bicycle. It seemed as if all my neighborhood friends had bikes, but not me. When we went to the department store to look at toys, I always wandered over to gaze at the bikes. They seemed to me to be bright and gleaming wonder machines. I dreamed of the places I would go and the adventures I would have if I just had a bike. I prayed for a bright red Schwinn, with white trim and big silver spokes.

Every time I mentioned my bike dream to my dad, he would tell me that he'd love to be able to buy me a bike, but he just couldn't afford it. As the fall arrived that particular year, I forced my bike dream into every conversation I could, until my poor frustrated father told me not to bring it up again. Christmas that year was the first Christmas in my life when I knew I would be disappointed, because I knew I wasn't getting the one thing I was convinced I couldn't live without, a brand-new bike. My younger brother and I opened small gift after small gift. These little toys were nice, but they were far from what I really wanted. Eventually there were no more beautifully wrapped gifts under the tree, and I tried to hide how disappointed I was. Thinking the gift-giving was over, we began to play with our toys. My dad left the room for a moment. I thought he was going to get a drink or a snack, but then out of the kitchen he came, rolling two bright shiny Schwinn bikes, one blue and white and one red and white. Tears welled up in my eyes as I ran over to grab my bike and to take in its beauty. Of course, I immediately asked, "Can we go ride them now?" as Mom and Dad laughed and said, "Maybe later."

Over the years I have been given many gifts by my loved ones, each one with special meaning of its own. Most of those gifts have been lost in time and memory. I have been given gifts that I asked for. I have been given gifts that people thought I would like or that I needed. I have been given gifts that didn't fit or didn't work properly. I have been given gifts that made me laugh and gifts that made me cry. I have been given gifts that confused me, leaving me wondering what the giver was thinking. But all of these gifts were given because the giver loved me.

But there is one gift I have been given that has changed me forever. For some years of my life, I didn't fully understand how much I needed this gift. This gift of gifts is not a thing, but a person. In fact, *the giver is the gift*; it is the gift of the Lord Jesus Christ. On one amazing night, in a stable in Bethlehem, the most wonderful gift that could ever be given was given to us. Although angels sang, shepherds worshiped, and Herod raged, for most of the world, this gift went unnoticed. The most remarkable gift that has ever been given, the one that would turn the world's sad story around, came through an unremarkable carpenter and his wife.

There was no appropriate place for the gift of gifts to be born. Here was the Lord, the Creator, taking on flesh so he could finally defeat the ultimate enemies of every human being, sin and death. Here was God offering his pleasing Son as our substitute in righteousness and sacrifice. Here was the light of lights, the Messiah,

the Savior, and the hope of the world. Here was the Wonderful
Counselor, the Mighty God, the Everlasting Father, and the Prince
of Peace. Here was the fulfillment of all the Old Testament promises of redemption. Here was the Son of God, Son of Man, seed
of David, and Immanuel. But, shockingly, there was no place for
him. There was no lavish palace, with a comfortable and beautiful
nursery, waiting for him. There was no reception committee, no
guards to protect him. There wasn't even an ordinary home for him.
There was no temporary hostel. Nothing had been prepared and
every place was full. The world wasn't waiting for him in anxious
anticipation. The world didn't stop in joyful celebration. In fact,
there wasn't even a place for the gift to lay his little infant head.
There didn't seem to be any room for him.

It is one of history's great paradoxes. There was no place for the
one gift that every human being desperately needs, whether they
know it or not. But it wasn't just at his birth that there was no
room. In the Savior's life, during his incarnate mission of love, as
predicted, he was despised and rejected, a man of sorrows. He was
quite acquainted with grief. People actually hid their faces from
the one who came to them on a mission of love (Isa. 53:3). He
came to lay down his life so they would have life, but they did not
receive him (John 1:11). I did it too. I once had no place for the
one whom I so deeply needed. There are times I still devalue the
gift of gifts and have no place for him, because other things have
become too valuable to me.

Corporate worship is designed to put the gift in front of us again
and again. It's meant to shine a bright light on his glory and his
grace. It's designed to cause us to examine whether the gift, Jesus,
still fills our hearts with overwhelming contentment and joy. It's
meant by God to warn us that no other gift can do in us, for us,

and through us what Jesus can do. And it's designed to take us back to that night and to that stable in Bethlehem, and ask once again, "Do you have room for him?"

———

Scripture: Luke 2:1–20

Reflections: Do other things sometimes become more valuable to you than the gift of gifts?

Family Discussion: Talk about some memorable gifts you've received in past years. What is your favorite part of the Christmas story?

Scripture Index

PAUL TRIPP MINISTRIES

Paul Tripp Ministries is a not-for-profit
organization connecting the transforming
power of Jesus Christ to everyday life. Hundreds
of resources are freely available online, on
social media, and on the Paul Tripp app.

PaulTripp.com

 /pdtripp   @paultripp   @paultrippquotes

Also Available from Paul David Tripp

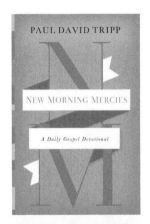

For more information, visit **crossway.org** or **paultripp.com**.